Floral ILLUSIONS
for **Quilters**

American Quilter's Society
P. O. Box 3290 • Paducah, KY 42002-3290
www.AQSquilt.com

Karen Combs

Located in Paducah, Kentucky, the American Quilter's Society (AQS) is dedicated to promoting the accomplishments of today's quilters. Through its publications and events, AQS strives to honor today's quiltmakers and their work and to inspire future creativity and innovation in quiltmaking.

EDITOR: MARJORIE L. RUSSELL

GRAPHIC DESIGN: AMY CHASE

COVER DESIGN: MICHAEL BUCKINGHAM

PHOTOGRAPHY: CHARLES R. LYNCH

HOW-TO- AND FLOWER PHOTOS: KAREN COMBS & BONNIE BROWNING

Library of Congress Cataloging-in-Publication Data

Combs, Karen

    Floral illusions for quilters / By Karen Combs

       p. cm.

    ISBN 1-57432-821-2

       1. Patchwork--Patterns.   2. Quilting--Patterns.   3. Flowers in art.

I. Title.

  TT835.C6487 2003

  746.46'041--dc21

             2003006525

Additional copies of this book may be ordered from the American Quilter's Society, PO Box 3290, Paducah, KY 42002-3290; 800-626-5420 (orders only please); or online at www.AQSquilt.com. For all other inquiries, call 270-898-7903.

Dedication

With love to my parents, J R "Jack" and Marvel Lippert, who instilled in me the value of hard work, the value of education, the desire to never give up, and the love of country. In memory of my father, Col. J R "Jack" Lippert (Colonel, United States Army, Retired) 1927–2003.

Acknowledgments

There are many people who supported and gave me encouragement during the two years it took to write this book. My thanks go to...

- Rick, my husband and best friend. Thank you for your love, encouragement, patience, support, and an occasional "Go get 'em!" All things seem possible with your help.

- my children, Angela and Josh, whose support and love mean the world to me. You both have grown to be fine, responsible, talented young adults. I'm very, very proud of you!

- the members of the Maury Quilter's Guild for their encouragement and support – in particular, to Lori Alspach, Sue Clark, Johnnie McCallum, Claire Sayer, and Ruth Spurlock, who willingly proofed patterns, tested directions, tested blocks, and made quilts. Your help was invaluable. I can't thank you enough!

- Barbie Kanta, who machine quilted many of the quilts in this book. Your talent for machine quilting makes my quilts shine. Thank you so much!

- Bill and Meredith Schroeder of the American Quilter's Society; plus Barbara Smith, executive book editor; Helen Squire; Marjorie Russell, my editor; and many others on the AQS staff. Thank you for your friendship, attention to detail, and the opportunity to work with you again.

Suppliers

Many companies have supplied products for this book. Special thanks are extended to:

- American & Efird, and Marci Brier for Mettler® and Signature® Threads

- Blank Textiles/Clearwater Fabrics and Bruce Magidson for fabric

- Pfaff USA for the 7570 Series Pfaff® Sewing Machine

- Prym Dritz®/Omnigrid for notions, rotary cutters, rulers, and mats

- Superior Threads and Heather Purcell for thread

Contents

Flowers are the poetry of earth,
as stars are the poetry of heaven.
      – Unknown

Introduction

Come forth into the light of things,
Let Nature be your teacher.

- *William Wordsworth, "The Tables Turned"*

Many of you know my work and may be asking, "Where are the cubes?" Since I love optical illusions in quilts, many of my quilt designs contain cubes and boxes of all sorts – hollow boxes, 3-D boxes, and boxes that create walls and corners all at the same time. I've always been fascinated with boxes and optical illusions. In this book, however, there are no boxes, but there are optical illusions.

It started out innocently enough. I was spending a great deal of time traveling and teaching. Often I found myself waiting around airports for delayed flights or spending hours flying to quilt guilds or quilt shows. I was not spending much time in my sewing room, and since I love designing and piecing quilts, I was getting crabby.

After thinking about my situation, I figured out the perfect solution and asked my husband to find me a new laptop. My requirements were that it be lightweight and have a long battery life. The rest was up to him. My computer guru husband rose to the challenge and found the perfect laptop, one weighing less than five pounds and with a battery life of up to four hours. To top it off, the screen was as large as the one on my home computer.

I was set. While waiting for planes, now I could create. In a matter of months, I had generated hundreds of quilt designs. I showed some of them to the editors at AQS and they loved them. The idea for *Floral Illusions* was born.

Why *Floral Illusions*? As I created designs, I found myself drawing pieced floral designs that just seemed to flow out of me. In fact, I could not get them recorded in my laptop fast enough. Perhaps it was because it was spring and I wanted to be in the garden planting flowers and herbs. Or perhaps the muse was screaming in my ear, "Do flower designs!" Whatever the reason, I found I had dozens of floral designs.

As I worked with the floral designs, I found I could place them in interesting settings and create illusions with the blocks. By setting the blocks in different ways, the illusions of motion and luminosity could be created. By playing with colors and shapes, secondary designs emerged as well. I had a great deal of fun designing these quilts and even more fun sewing them. I hope you will as well.

Some of the blocks are pieced using traditional methods, some are rotary cut, and some are paper pieced.

Let me share a secret with you: I never liked paper piecing. I tried it years ago, but did not like it. Still, I was fascinated by the possibilities of paper piecing and loved the idea of making very difficult angles or precise points with ease. As I designed quilts for this book, I realized paper piecing would be an excellent method to create some of these quilts.

I knew I had to find a way to enjoy paper piecing. In fact, as I showed students in my classes these new designs, someone asked how I was going to make them. "Paper piecing," I replied, and several students groaned. One asked, "Do you like paper piecing?" "No," I responded, then added, "but I am going to find a way to like it!" Several students smiled as I was told, "When you find it, let us know."

Well, I have found a way to like paper piecing. I guess you could say I really love it! In this book, I'm going to show you a way to paper piece that is easier, quicker, and (can it be true?) seam ripper free!

I've also included dozens of my own photographs of flowers and gardens in this book. I love to take photos and enjoy photographing gardens, scenery, and flowers. I hope you will enjoy looking at them as much as I do.

Enjoy your Floral Illusions!

Karen

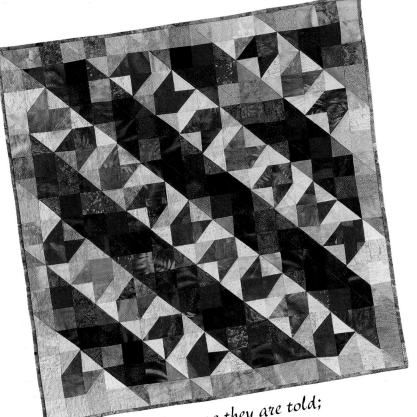

Here tulips bloom as they are told;
Unkempt about those hedges blows
An English unofficial rose...
- Rupert Brooke, "The Old Vicarage, Grantchester"

Rated
Easy

Sewing method
Traditional piecing

Quilt size
34" x 34"

Pieced Block

Tulip

Springtime Tulips

Colorful tulips cascade across the surface of this scrappy quilt with an illusion of motion. I used blue, orange, and cream for my scraps, but you can use your favorite colors.

Fabrics

Blocks

Assorted dark and medium blue scraps (blue, teal, blue-violet)

Assorted light scraps (white, off-white, light yellow, very light blue)

Assorted medium orange scraps (yellow, orange, red, red-orange, red-violet)

Borders

Assorted light scraps (blue, yellow, cream)

Binding

Light blue batik   ⅓ yard

Tulip
Make 25
Finished size: 6"

Make 25 Tulip blocks as shown (Fig. 1). Be sure to use a variety of scraps in each block. After sewing together 3" half-square triangle units, trim to 2½".

Cutting for Tulip blocks

◪ *Cut square in half diagonally.*

Fabric	Cut pieces	Dimensions
Dark and medium blue scraps		
(blue, teal, blue-violet)	75	2½" x 2½"
	38 ◪	3" x 3"
Light scraps		
(white, off-white, light yellow, very light blue)	63 ◪	3" x 3"
Medium orange scraps		
(yellow, orange, red, red-orange, red-violet)	25	2½" x 2½"
	25 ◪	3" x 3"

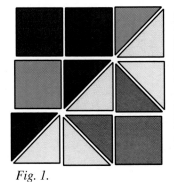 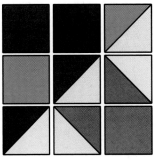 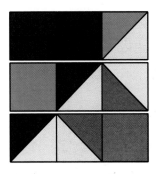 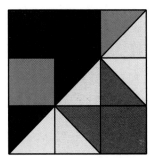

Fig. 1.   *Make 25.*

Quilt Top Assembly

Arrange blocks as shown (Fig. 2, page 8). Sew blocks into horizontal rows and then join the rows.

Arrange squares and triangles as shown in figure 3. After sewing together 3" half-square triangle units, trim to 2½".

Sew together squares and triangles as shown into border strips. Sew border strips to the sides of the quilt top, then to the top and bottom. (Fig. 3).

Layer your quilt top with batting and backing; baste (refer to Finishing, Pg. 105).

Border Squares and Binding
Cutting for borders and binding

⧄ *Cut square in half diagonally.*

Fabric	Cut pieces	Dimensions
Light blue	23	2½" x 2½"
	9 ⧄	3" x 3"
Light yellow and/or off-white	22	2½" x 2½"
	9 ⧄	3" x 3"
Light blue batik	4	2" x 44"
	(Make continuous binding as shown on pages 106–107.)	

Quilting

SPRINGTIME TULIP was stipple quilted around the tulip shapes using a light colored thread. Then it was quilted in diagonal lines with dark thread in the dark areas. After quilting, bind the edges, and label your quilt.

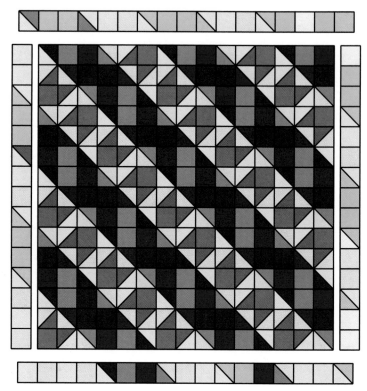

Fig. 2.

Fig. 3.

Rated
Easy

Sewing method
Traditional piecing

Quilt size
36" x 36"

Pieced Blocks

Posy

Triangle

Sweet spring, full of sweet days and roses...
- George Herbert, "Virtue"

Ring Around the Posy

The posies in this fun, but easy, design appear to move around the quilt. Do you notice how the Posy blocks create a star in the center of the quilt? Choose bright colors with a black background for a different look. Quilted by Barbie Kanta.

Fabrics

Blocks

Cream	1 yard
Purple	¼ yard
Light green	¼ yard
Dark blue	½ yard
Dark pink	¼ yard
Dark green	¼ yard
Medium blue	¼ yard

Binding

Dark blue	⅓ yard

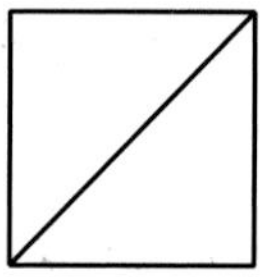

Triangle
Make 20
Finished size: 6"

Cutting for Triangle blocks

Fabric	Cut pieces	Dimensions
Cream	10	7" x 7"
Dark blue	10	7" x 7"

  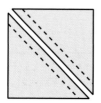

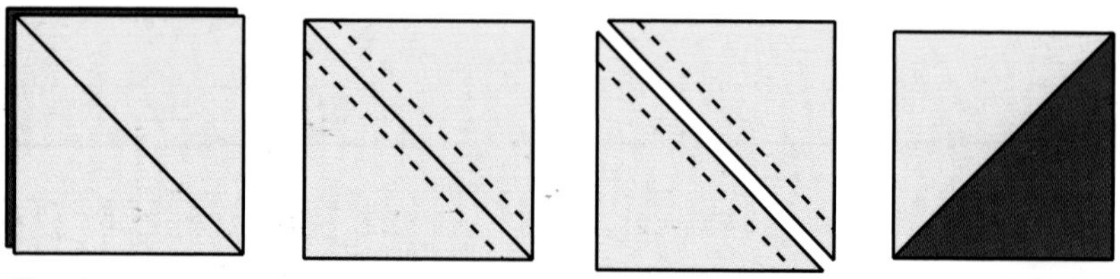

Fig. 1.

Make 20.

Make 20 Triangle blocks by placing each of ten 7" cream squares, right sides together, with a 7" dark blue square (Fig. 1). Draw a line from corner to corner. Sew ¼" away from either side of the line. Cut on the drawn line. Press open and trim each square to 6½".

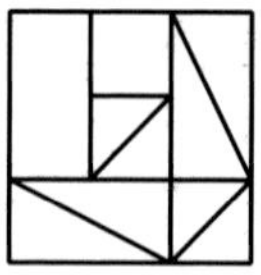

Posy
Make 16
Finished size: 6"

Cutting for Posy blocks

Fabric	Cut pieces	Dimensions
Cream	16	2½" x 4½"
	16	2½" x 2½"
	16	2¾" x 5⅛"
Pink	8	3" x 3"
Medium blue	8	3" x 3"
Purple	8	3" x 3"
Light green	8	3" x 3"
Dark green	16	2¾" x 5⅛"

Make 16 half-square triangle units in the same way the Triangle blocks were made in figure 1. Place each of eight pink 3" squares, right sides together, with a medium blue 3" square. Draw a line from corner to corner. Sew ¼" away from either side of the line. Cut on the drawn line. Press and trim squares to 2½" (Fig. 2).

Fig. 2.
Make 16.

Fig. 3.
Make 16.

As in figure 1, make 16 half-square triangle units by placing each of eight purple 3" squares, right sides together, with a light green 3" square. Draw a line from corner to corner. Sew ¼" away from either side of the line. Cut on the drawn line. Press and trim squares to 2½" (Fig. 3).

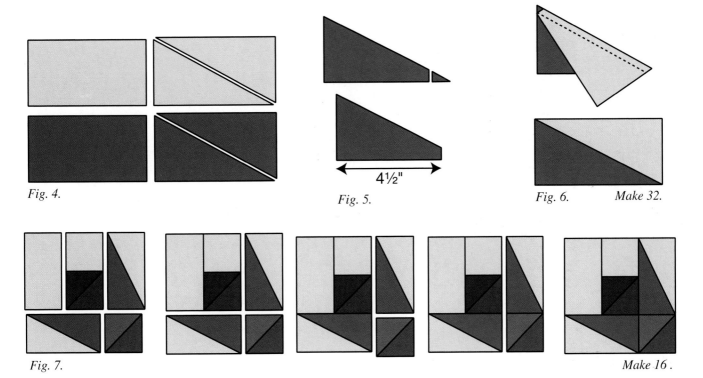

Fig. 4.

Fig. 5.

Fig. 6.   Make 32.

Fig. 7.

Make 16.

To make 32 rectangle units that are half dark green and half cream, first cut each of sixteen 2¾" x 5⅛" dark green rectangles and cream rectangles from corner to corner as shown (Fig. 4).

Trim the tip of each half rectangle at the 4½" point to blunt the end (Fig. 5). This will make it easier to piece the patches.

Assemble the rectangle units as shown (Fig. 6).

Assemble 16 Posy blocks in units as shown (Fig. 7).

Fig. 8. Quilt assembly.

Quilt Top Assembly

Arrange Posy blocks and Triangle blocks as shown (Fig. 8). Sew blocks into horizontal rows and then join the rows.

Fig. 9. Alternate design #1.

Fig. 10. Alternate design #2.

Fig. 11. Alternate design #3.

Cutting for Binding

Cut four strips, 2" x 44", from dark blue fabric. Make continuous binding as shown on pages 106–107.

Layer your quilt top with batting and backing; baste (refer to Finishing on page 105).

Quilting

Barbie Kanta, a longarm machine quilter, quilted lovely flowing shapes in the light areas and in the flowers of RING AROUND THE POSY. You could also stipple quilt the light areas and outline quilt the dark areas and the flowers. After quilting, bind the edges and label your quilt.

RING AROUND THE POSY
Alternate Designs

Create some different designs by rotating the blocks (Figs. 9-11). It's amazing how they can change with just a flick of the wrist.

Rated

Easy

Sewing methods

Paper piecing and traditional piecing

Quilt size

43" x 43"

Paper Pieced Block

Peony

Pieced Block

Triangle

Come gentle Spring! ethereal Mildness! Come.
- James Thomson, "The Seasons"

Amish Spring

The traditional Amish quilt design, Shoo Fly, inspired the secondary design in this lovely springtime quilt. Use gradated fabrics in the Peony block for an interesting look.

Fabrics

Blocks

Light blue	1¼ yard
Dark blue	¾ yard
Light orange	½ yard
Medium green	¼ yard
Dark green	½ yard
Purples (gradated)	
#1 Light purple	¼ yard
#2 Medium light purple	¼ yard
#3 Medium purple	⅜ yard
#4 Medium dark purple	⅜ yard
#5 Dark purple	⅓ yard

Borders & Binding

Light orange	⅓ yard
Dark blue	1 yard

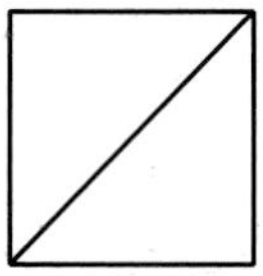

Triangle
Make 8
Finished size: 6"

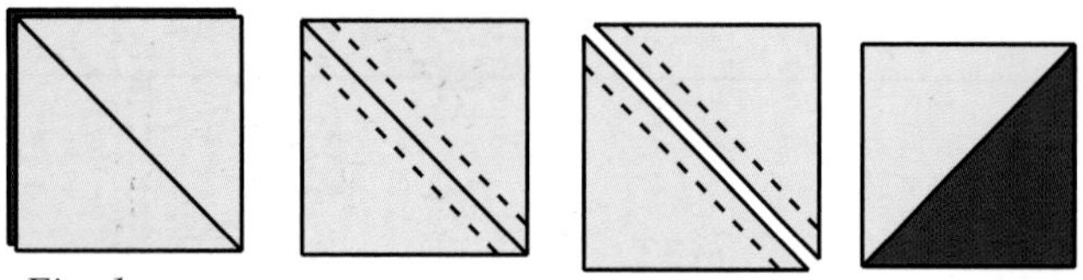

Fig. 1.   *Make 8.*

Fig. 2. Make 12.

Cutting for Triangle blocks

Fabric	Cut pieces	Dimensions
Dark blue	10	7" x 7"
Orange	6	7" x 7"
Light blue	4	7" x 7"

Make eight Triangle blocks by placing four 7" light blue squares, right sides together, with four 7" dark blue squares (Fig. 1). Draw a line from corner to corner. Sew ¼" away from either side of the line. Cut on the drawn line. Press open and trim each square to 6½".

Make 12 Triangle blocks by placing six 7" orange squares, right sides together, with six 7" dark blue squares (Fig. 2). Draw a line from corner to corner. Sew ¼" away from either side of the line. Cut on the drawn line. Press open and trim each square to 6½".

Peony
Make 16
Finished size: 6"

Make 16 paper copies of the four pattern units on page 17. Cut out ½" beyond the outside lines.

Cutting for Peony blocks

Fabric	Cut pieces	Dimensions	Unit, Location
Light blue	80	2½" x 2½"	A1, A4, A6, B2, C2
	32	2¼" x 5¼"	B3, D4
Dark green	32	2¼" x 5¼"	B4, D3
	16	2½" x 2½"	D2
Medium green	16	2½" x 2½"	D1
Purples			
#1 Light	16	2½" x 2½"	A2
#2 Medium light	16	2½" x 2½"	A3
#3 Medium	16	2¼" x 3¾"	A5
#4 Medium dark	16	2¼" x 3¾"	C1
#5 Dark	16	2¼" x 5¼"	B1

Make blocks, placing fabrics as shown (Fig. 3). To form a block, join
Unit A to Unit C; join Unit AC to Unit B; then join Unit ABC to Unit D.

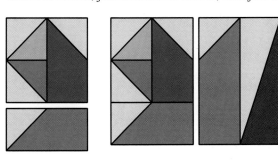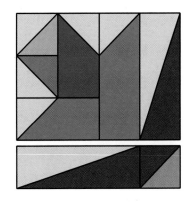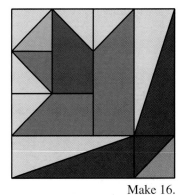

Fig. 3.

Make 16.

Quilt Top Assembly

Arrange blocks as shown (Fig. 4). Sew blocks into horizontal rows and then join the rows.

Fig. 4. Quilt assembly.

Fig. 5.

Borders and Binding

Cutting for borders and binding

Fabric	Cut pieces	Dimensions	Location
Orange	2	1½" x 36½"	Inner side borders
	2	1½" x 38"	Inner top and bottom borders
Dark blue	2	3½" x 38½"	Side borders
	2	3½" x 44½"	Top and bottom borders
Dark blue	5	2" x 44"	Binding (Make continuous binding as shown on pages 106–107.)

Sew inner border strips to the sides of the quilt top (Fig. 5), then to the top and bottom (refer to border instructions on Pages 103–104). Repeat with the outer borders.

Layer your quilt top with batting and backing; then baste (see Finishing, page 105).

Quilting

AMISH SPRING was stipple quilted using white thread in the white area, dark blue in the dark blue area, and yellow thread in the yellow area. The leaves and flowers were outline quilted. After quilting, bind the edges and label your quilt.

AMISH SPRING *Alternate Designs*

Believe it or not, the alternate designs (Figs. 6 and 7) are created using the same blocks. By turning the blocks you can create either of the designs below.

Fig. 6. Alternate design #1.

Fig. 7. Alternate design #2.

ORANGE SHERBET, 45" x 45", Johnnie McCallum, Columbia, Tennessee. Johnnie used bright, warm colors in her version of the AMISH SPRING quilt. These colors create a cheerful and vibrant quilt.

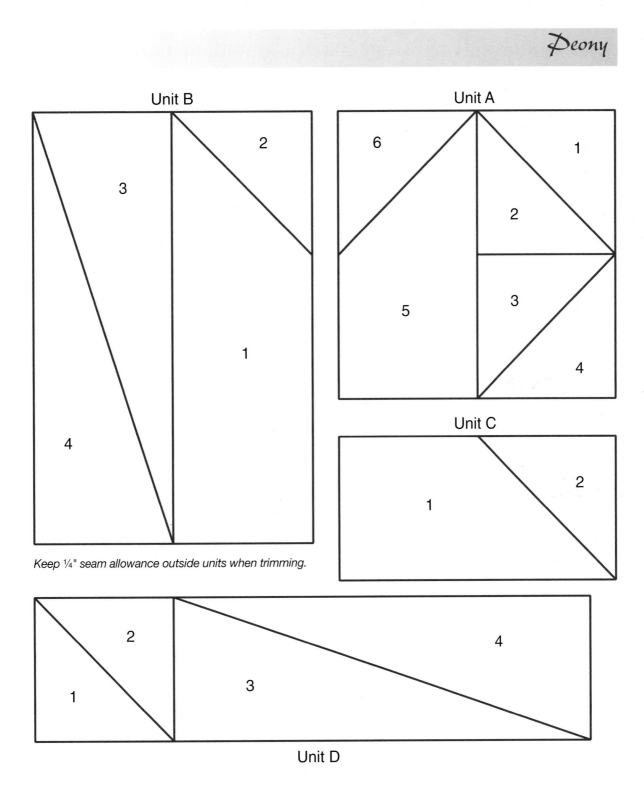

Unit B

Unit A

Unit C

Keep ¼" seam allowance outside units when trimming.

Unit D

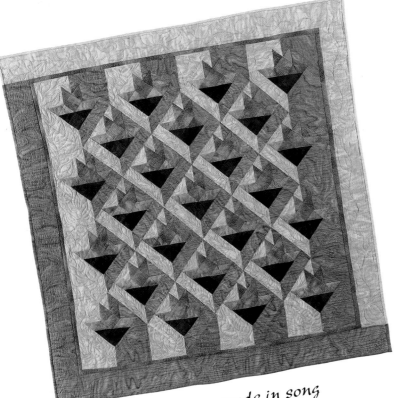

If I could put my woods in song
And tell what's there enjoyed,
All men would to my garden throng,
And leave the cities void.
- Ralph Waldo Emerson, "My Garden"

Rated
Easy

Sewing method
Traditional piecing

Quilt size
40" x 40"

Pieced Block

Rose

Waterlilies

This is a fun quilt with rows of flowers that create an illusion of motion. The light and dark blue background creates a complex design, but it is easy to sew. *Quilted by Barbie Kanta.*

Fabrics

Blocks, Borders, and Binding

Pink	½ yard
Yellow	½ yard
Dark green	½ yard
Light blue	1 yard
Dark blue	1 yard

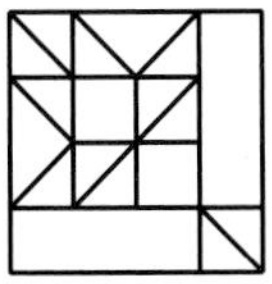

Rose
Make 25
Finished size: 6"

Make 50 half-square triangle units by placing each of 25, 2⅜" light blue squares, right sides together, with a 2⅜" dark blue square (Fig. 1). Draw a line from corner to corner. Sew ¼" away from either side of the line. Cut on the drawn line. Press and trim squares to 2".

Cutting for Rose blocks

Fabric	Cut pieces	Dimensions
Pink	75	2" x 2"
Green	25	2" x 2"
	25	2⅜" x 2⅜"
Yellow	50	2" x 2"
	25	2⅜" x 2⅜"
Light blue	25	2⅜" x 2⅜"
	25	2" x 3½"
	25	2" x 5"
Dark blue	25	2⅜" x 2⅜"
	25	2" x 3½"
	25	2" x 5"

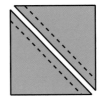

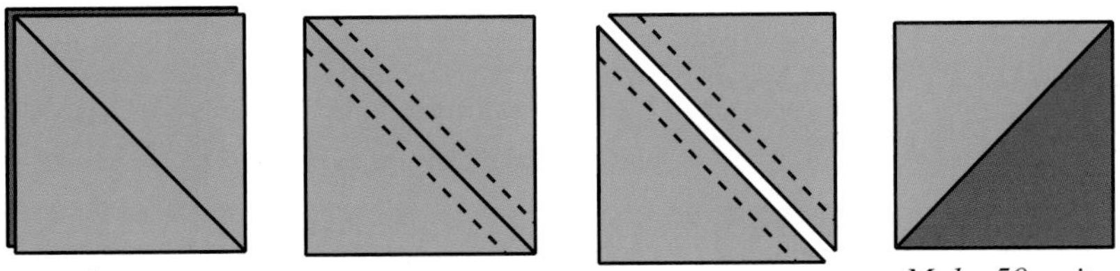

Fig. 1.   *Make 50 units.*

Make 50 half-square triangle units as shown above, by placing each of 25, 2⅜" yellow squares, right sides together, with a 2⅜" green square (Fig. 2). Draw a line from corner to corner. Sew ¼" away from either side of the line. Cut on the drawn line. Press and trim the squares to 2".

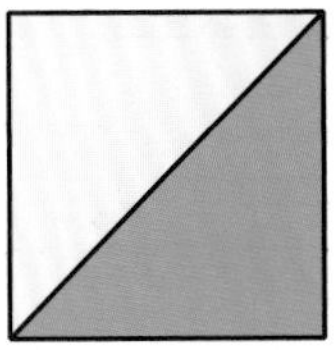

Fig. 2.
Make 50 units.

Waterlilies

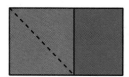    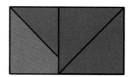

Fig. 3.

Make 25 units.

Make 25 rectangle units (some call them Flying Geese units) as shown in figure 3.

Draw a line diagonally from corner to corner on the wrong side of 50 of the 2" pink squares.

Fig. 4.
Make 25 units.

Place a pink square on a 2" x 3½" dark blue rectangle as shown. Sew on the line. Using a rotary cutter and ruler, trim ¼" from the stitching line. Press the patch open.

Draw a line diagonally from corner to corner on the wrong side of 50 of the 2" green squares. Repeat, sewing a green square to the other end of the rectangle. The two squares will overlap at the middle top. When the units are sewn into the block, this overlap will be in the seam allowance and you will have a crisp point. Make 25.

Repeat the above instructions using light blue rectangles (Fig. 4). Make 25 units.

Assemble 25 Rose blocks as shown below (Fig. 5).

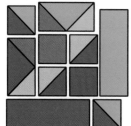 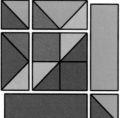 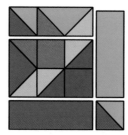 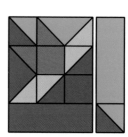 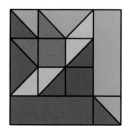

Fig. 5.

Make 25.

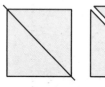

Corner Triangles

From light blue fabric, cut one 5⅛" square and cut into triangles as shown (Fig. 6). Repeat with dark blue fabric. These will be placed on the corners of the quilt. (Only two light triangles and two dark triangles will be used. You will have two light and two dark triangles left over.)

Top and Bottom Triangles

From light blue fabric, cut two 5⅛" squares and cut into triangles as shown (Fig. 7). Repeat with dark blue fabric.

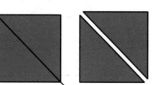

Fig. 6.

After cutting, sew light and dark units together as shown (Fig. 8). These will be placed on the top and bottom of the quilt.

Fig. 8a. Make 3.

Side Triangles

From dark blue fabric, cut one 9½" square and cut into triangles as shown (Fig. 9, page 21). Repeat with light blue fabric. These will be placed on the sides of the quilt. (Only three of the four units will be used in the quilt. You will have one light and one dark triangle left over.)

Fig. 7.

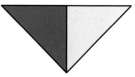

Fig. 8b. Make 3.

Quilt Top Assembly

Arrange Rose blocks and border triangles as shown (Fig. 10). Sew blocks in diagonal rows.

Fig. 9.

9" triangles on sides

5⅛" triangles on corners

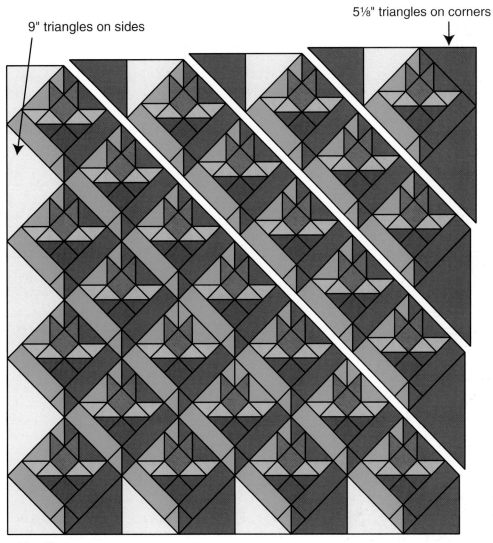

Fig. 10.

Borders and Binding
Cutting for borders and binding

Fabric	Cut pieces	Dimensions	Location
Pink	4	1½" x 44	Inner border
Light blue	2	3½" x 44"	Outer border
Medium blue	2	3½" x 44"	Outer border
Light blue batik	5	2" x 44"	Binding

(Make continuous binding as shown on pages 106–107.)

Sew inner border strips to the sides of the quilt top (Fig. 11), then to the top and bottom (refer to border information on pages 103–104).

Repeat with the outer borders. Sew the light blue to the right side of the quilt, and the medium blue to the left side of the quilt. Then, sew the light blue to the top of the quilt and the medium blue to the bottom of the quilt.

Layer your quilt top with batting and backing; baste (refer to Finishing on page 105).

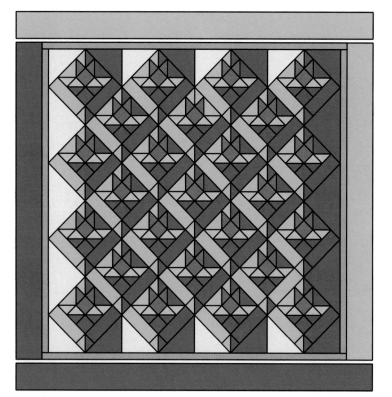

Fig. 11.

Quilting

Longarm machine quilter, Barbie Kanta, quilted vines and leaves in the light blue areas and shapes like ripples in the darker blue areas of WATERLILIES. Another option would be to outline quilt the waterlilies and stipple quilt the borders. After quilting, bind the edges and label your quilt.

WATERLILIES
Alternate Designs

Change the look and illusions by re-arranging the blocks and setting triangles (Fig. 12 and 13.

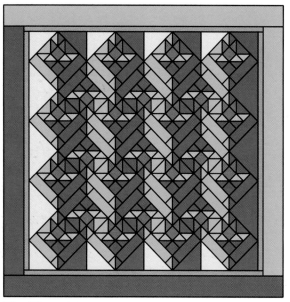

Fig. 12.

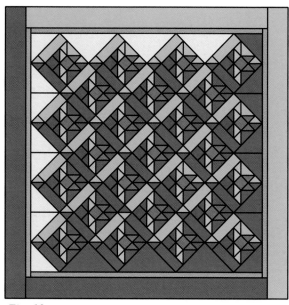

Fig. 13.

Rated
Intermediate

Sewing method
Paper piecing
Traditional piecing

Quilt size
46" x 46"

Paper Pieced Block

Snow Drop

Pieced Block

Triangle

Shining through tears, like April suns in showers,...

- Thomas Otway, "Venice Preserved"

Tear Drops

I designed this quilt to make a secondary Churn Dash design appear in the background. On September 11, 2001, I was selecting bright, colorful fabrics for this quilt, but after seeing the attacks on the World Trade Center and the Pentagon, I changed to more somber colors. I shed many tears as I pieced this quilt, thus the name.

Fabrics

Blocks

Light blue	⅓ yard
Medium blue	¼ yard
Dark blue	¾ yard
Medium/light green	¼ yard
Medium green	⅓ yard
Dark green	¼ yard
Ivory	2 yards

Borders and Binding

Dark green	½ yard
Medium blue	1 yard

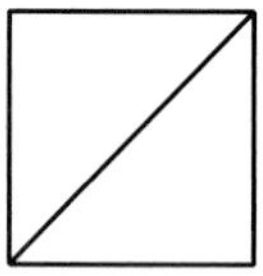

Triangle
Make 12
Finished size: 6"

Make 12 triangle blocks by placing six 7" light blue squares, right sides together, with six 7" dark blue squares. Draw a line from corner to corner (Fig. 1). Sew ¼" away from either side of the line. Cut on the drawn line. Press open and trim squares to 6½".

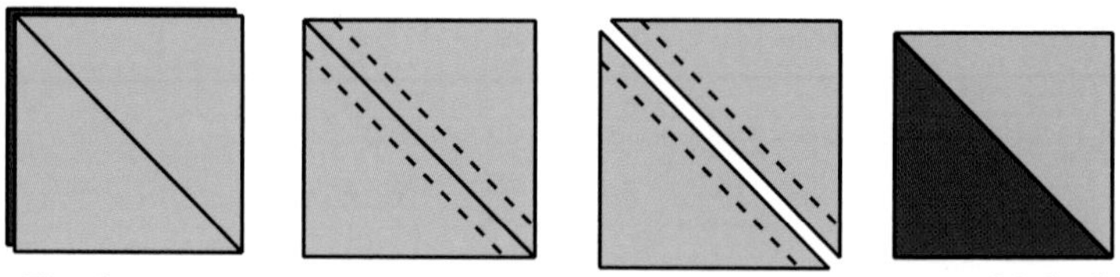

Cutting for Triangle blocks

Fabric	Cut pieces	Dimensions
Dark blue	6	7" x 7"
Light blue	6	7" x 7"

Fig. 1.   *Make 12.*

Snow Drop
Make 24*
Finished size: 6"

*See below for color variations.

Make 24 paper copies of the pattern on page 27. Cut out ½" beyond the outside lines.

Cutting for Snow Drop blocks
Cut square in half diagonally.

Fabric	Cut pieces	Dimensions	Location
Medium light green	24	1¼" x 1¼"	1
Medium green	24	2½" x 4"	8
Dark green	24	2¾" x 5"	9
Ivory	48	2½" x 2½"	2, 3
	24	2¾" x 4"	6
	24	2½" x 3¾"	7
	48	2½" x 5½"	10, 11
	32	4" x 4"	12, 13, 14, 15
Medium blue	24	2½" x 2½"	4
Dark blue	24	3½" x 5"	5
	16	5" x 5"	12, 13, 14, 15

Make blocks, placing fabrics as shown (Fig. 2).

Fig. 2a.   *Make 8.*   *Fig. 2b.*   *Make 16.*

Quilt Top Assembly

Arrange blocks as shown (Fig. 3). Sew blocks into
horizontal rows and then join the rows.

Fig. 3.

Fig. 4.

Borders and Binding

Cutting for borders and binding

Fabric	Cut pieces	Dimensions	Location
Dark green	2	1½" x 36½"	Side borders
	2	1½" x 38"	Top and bottom borders
Medium blue	2	4½" x 37½"	Side borders
	3	4½" x 44"	Top and bottom borders
Medium blue	5	2" x 44"	Binding
		(Make continuous binding as shown on pages 106–107.)	

Sew inner border strips to the top and bottom of the quilt top (Fig. 4), then to the
sides (refer to border information on pages 103–104). Repeat with the outer borders.
Top and bottom borders will need to be pieced.

Layer your quilt top with batting and backing; baste (refer to Finishing, page 105).

Quilting

TEAR DROPS was stipple quilted using a light thread in the light areas. Diagonal
lines in dark blue thread were quilted along the outside triangles and in the border.
After quilting, bind the edges and make a label for your quilt.

TEAR DROPS *Alternate Designs*

Fig. 5. Alternate design #1.

Fig. 6. Alternate design #2.

Fig. 7. Alternate design #3.

Fig. 8. Alternate design #4.

See how the look changes when the blocks are rearranged (Fig. 5-8).

I THINK IT NEEDS RED, *36" x 36". Resa Beasley of Columbia, Tennessee, created this Tear Drops variation using alternate design #4. The monochromatic color scheme is striking.*

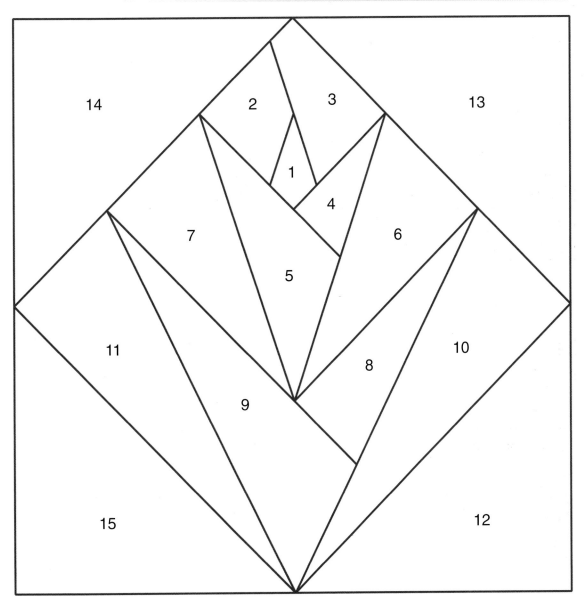

Snow Drop

Keep ¼" seam allowance outside block when trimming.

Rated
Intermediate

Sewing method
Paper piecing

Quilt size
44" x 44"

Paper Pieced Blocks

Bird of Paradise

Prickly Pear

The handsomest and most interesting flowers were the great purple orchises... with their great purple spikes perfectly erect, amid the shrubs and grasses of the shore.
- Henry David Thoreau, "The Maine Woods"

Star Flower

Two blocks combine to create the illusion of motion and to create stars among the bird-of-paradise flowers.

Fabrics

Blocks, Borders, and Binding

White	1¼ yard
Light pink	¾ yard
Dark pink	¾ yard
Light green	⅓ yard
Dark green	½ yard
Red violet	¼ yard
Blue	½ yard

Blocks and Binding

White	¼ yard
Blue	¾ yard

Bird of Paradise
Make 20
Finished size: 6"

Make 20 paper copies of both pattern units on page 32. Cut out ½" beyond the outside lines.

Cutting for Bird of Paradise blocks

Fabric	Cut pieces	Dimensions	Unit, Location
White	40	3¼"x 5"	A1, B1
	40	2¾" x 6¼"	A5, B5
Light green	40	1½" x 4"	A2, B2
Dark green	40	2" x 7¼"	A4, B4
Light pink	20	2½" x 8"	A3
Dark pink	20	2½" x 8"	B3

Make 20 blocks, placing fabrics as shown, and sewing Unit A to Unit B for each block (Fig. 1).

Fig. 1.

Make 20.

Prickly Pear
Make 16
Finished size: 6"

Make 16 paper copies of both pattern units on this page. Cut out ½" beyond the outside lines.

Make 16 blocks, placing fabrics as shown, sewing Unit A to Unit B for each block (Fig. 2).

Cutting for Prickly Pear blocks

Fabric	Cut pieces	Dimensions	Unit, Location
White	32	2" x 7¼"	A1, B1
Red-violet	32	1¼" x 5¾"	A2, B2
Blue	32	3½" x 5"	A3, B3
Purple	32	3" x 10"	A4, B4

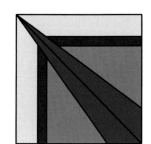

Fig. 2.   Make 16.

Prickly Pear

Unit B

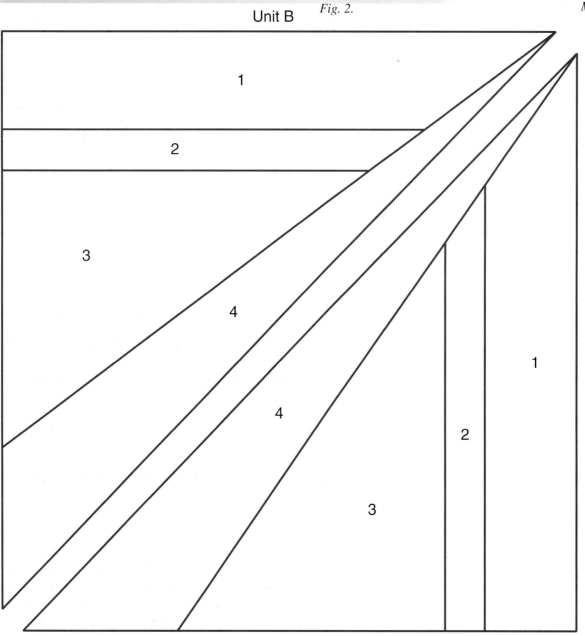

Keep ¼" seam allowance outside units when trimming.

Unit A

Quilt Top Assembly

Arrange blocks as shown (Fig. 3). Sew blocks into horizontal rows and then join the rows.

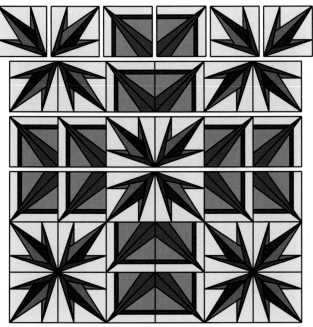

Fig. 3.

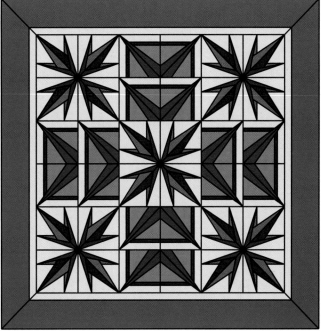

Fig. 4.

Borders and Binding

Cutting for borders and binding

Fabric	Cut pieces	Dimensions	Location
White	4	1½" x 44"	Top, bottom, right, left sides
Blue	4	3½" x 44"	Top, bottom, right, left sides
Blue	5	2" x 44"	Binding
			Make continuous binding as shown on pages 106–107.)

Sew the white inner border and blue outer border strips together, matching the centers. Press the seams toward the blue border.

Attach the borders and miter the each corner of the quilt (Fig. 4) following the mitering instructions on page 104.

Layer your quilt top with batting and backing; baste (refer to Finishing, page 105).

Quilting

STAR FLOWER was stipple quilted using a white thread in the white area and medium blue in the blue areas. The purple spikes were outline quilted. Flowers and leaves were purposely not quilted so the stippling surrounding them would puff them up for an almost three-dimensional look. After quilting, bind the edges and label your quilt.

Bird of Paradise

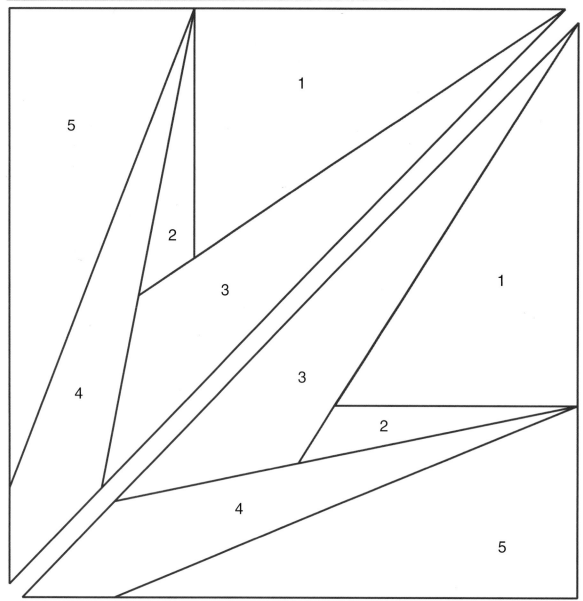

Unit B

1

5

2

3

3

1

2

4

4

5

Keep ¼" seam allowance outside units when trimming.

Unit A

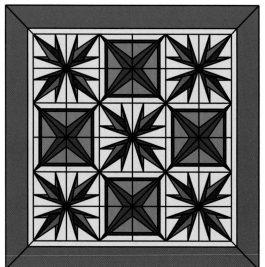

STAR FLOWER
Alternate Designs

Re-arrange the blocks and an entirely new design emerges (Fig. 5).

Fig. 5. Alternate design.

Rated

Intermediate

Sewing methods

Paper piecing
Traditional piecing

Quilt size

46" x 46"

Paper Pieced Block

Bird of Paradise

Pieced Block

Corner

The teeming autumn big with rich increase...
- William Shakespeare, "Sonnet XCVII"

Star Glow

I love the illusions of curves that are created by these blocks. I found the border fabric for this quilt first and then selected the rest of the fabrics to coordinate with the border fabric.

Fabrics

Blocks

Ivory	1 yard
Medium green	⅓ yard
Light green	1½ yards
Dark green	1¼ yards
Medium red	1¼ yards
Dark red	1¼ yards

Borders and Binding

Gold	½ yard
Leaf print	¾ yard*

*(includes binding)

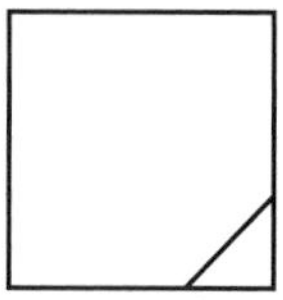

Corner
Make 4
Finished size: 6"

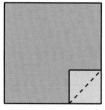

Fig. 1.

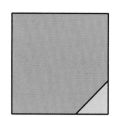

Make 4.

Cutting for Corner blocks

Fabric	Cut pieces	Dimensions
Light green	4	6½" x 6½"
Ivory	4	2½"

Make four Corner blocks by placing one 2½" ivory square, right sides together, on one corner of each 6½" light green square (Fig. 1). Draw a line from corner to corner and sew on the line. Press the ivory square toward the corner and cut away the excess fabric on the back, ¼" from the seam.

Bird of Paradise
Make 32*
Finished size: 6"

*See figure 2 for color variations.

Make 32 paper copies of both pattern units on page 35. Cut out ½" beyond the outside lines.

Make blocks, placing fabrics as shown (Fig. 2).

Cutting for Bird of Paradise blocks

Fabric	Cut pieces	Dimensions	Location
Medium green	64	1½" x 4"	A2, B2
Dark green	64	2" x 7¼"	A4, B4
Medium red	32	2½" x 8"	B3
Dark red	32	2½" x 8"	A3
Cream	12	3¼" x 5"	A1
	12	3¼" x 5"	B1
	32	2¾" x 6¼"	A5, B5
Light green	20	3¼" x 5"	A1
	20	3¼" x 5"	B1
	32	2¾" x 6¼"	A5, B5

Fig. 2a. Make 4.

Fig. 2b. Make 4.

Fig. 2c. Make 4.

Fig. 2d. Make 4.

Fig. 2e. Make 8.

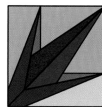

Fig. 2f. Make 8.

Bird of Paradise

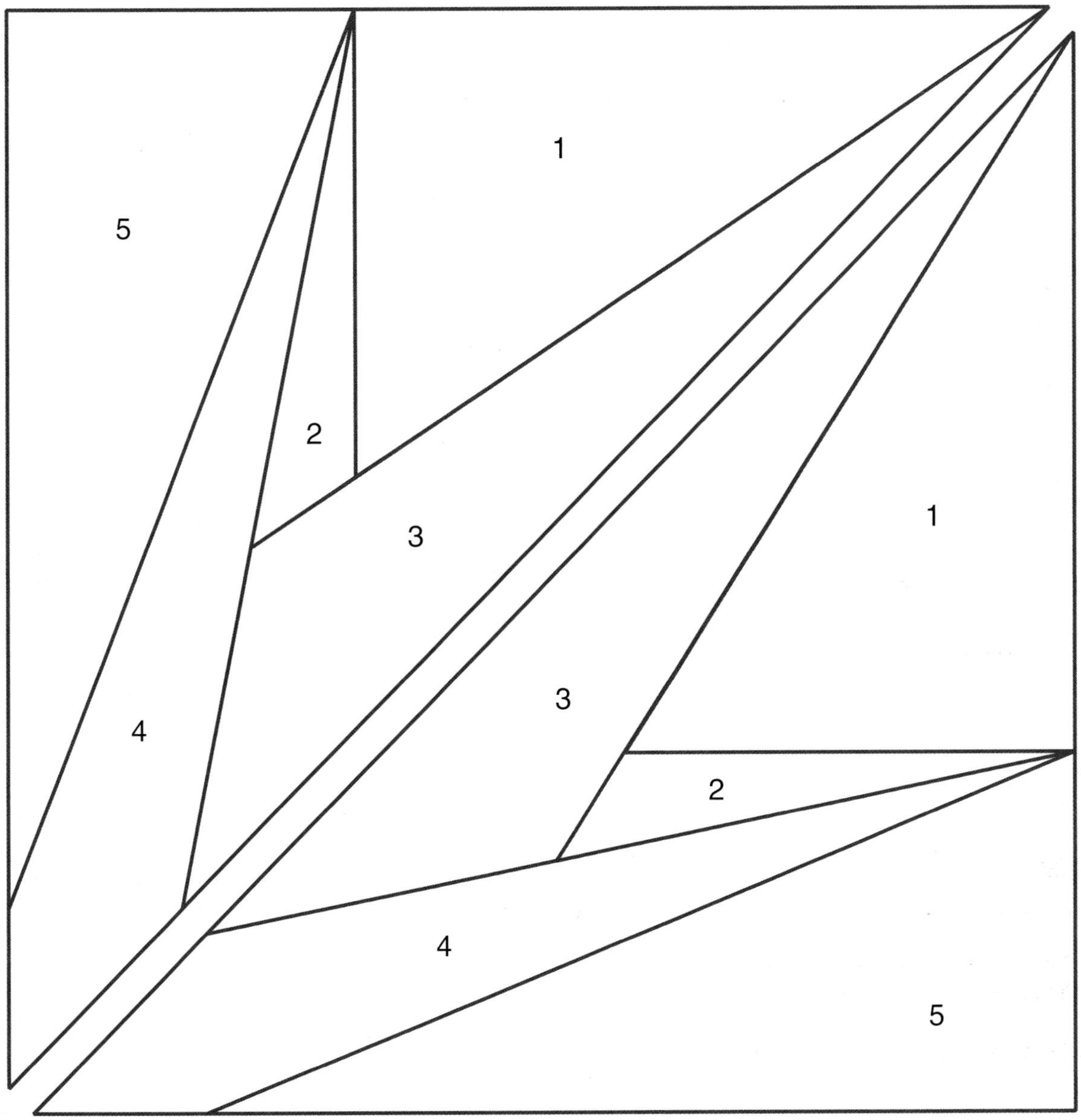

Unit B

5

1

2

3

1

4

3

2

4

5

Keep ¼" seam allowance outside units when trimming.

Unit A

Quilt Top Assembly

Arrange blocks as shown (Fig. 3). Sew blocks into horizontal rows and then join the rows.

Fig. 3.

Borders and Binding

Cutting for borders and binding

Fabric	Cut pieces	Dimensions	Location
Gold	2	1½" x 36½"	Inner side borders
	2	1½" x 38"	Inner top and bottom borders
Leaf print	2	4½" x 37½"	Side borders
	3	4½" x 44"	Top and bottom borders
Leaf print	5	2" x 44"	Binding

(Make continuous binding as shown on pages 106–107.)

Sew inner border strips to the top and bottom of the quilt top (Fig. 4), then to the sides (refer to border information on pages 103–104). Repeat with the outer borders. Top and bottom borders will need to be pieced/

Layer your quilt top with batting and backing; baste (refer to Finishing, page 105).

Quilting

The Bird of Paradise blocks in STAR GLOW were outline quilted, while the green and cream background areas were stipple quilted. After quilting, bind the edges and make a label for your quilt.

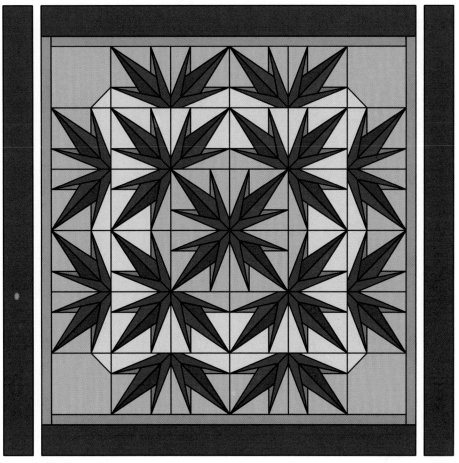

Fig. 4.

STAR GLOW *Alternate Designs*

Simply reversing the outer blocks gives this design (Fig. 5) a different look, in which plain squares replace corner squares.

Fig. 5. Alternate design.

"The shows of the day, the dewy morning, the rainbow, mountains, orchards in blossom, stars, moonlight, shadows in still water, and the like…"

- Ralph Waldo Emerson, "Nature"

Rated
Intermediate

Sewing methods
Paper piecing
Traditional piecing

Quilt size
48" x 48"

Paper Pieced Block

Palm

Pieced Block

Triangle

Plain Block

Plain

Spider Webs and Fairy Flowers

Just three blocks create a dramatic, yet delicate, design with an illusion of motion. Batiks or marbled fabrics add a special touch to this quilt. *Quilted by Barbie Kanta.*

Fabrics

Blocks, Borders, and Binding

Light tone-on-tone green	½ yard
Medium tone-on-tone green	¾ yard
Dark tone-on-tone green	1 yard
Light cream batik	1¾ yard
Medium blue batik	2 yards

Plain
Make 4
Finished Size: 6"

Cutting for Plain blocks

Fabric	Cut pieces	Dimensions
Light cream batik	4	6½" x 6½"

Triangle
Make 12
Finished size: 6"

Cutting for Triangle blocks

Fabric	Cut pieces	Dimensions
Light batik	6	7" x 7"
Blue batik	6	7" x 7"

Make 12 Triangle blocks by placing each of six 7" light cream batik squares, right sides together, with a 7" blue batik square (Fig. 1). Draw a line from corner to corner. Sew ¼" away from either side of the line. Cut on the drawn line. Press open and trim each square to 6½".

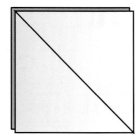 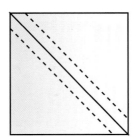 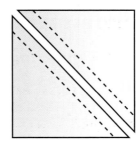 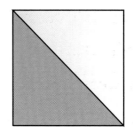

Fig. 1.

Make 12.

Palm
Make 20*
Finished size: 6"

*See below for color variations.

Make 20 paper copies of both pattern units on page 44. Cut out ½" beyond the outside lines.

Make blocks in the colorways as shown (Fig. 2), connecting Unit A to Unit B.

Cutting for Palm blocks

Fabric	Cut pieces	Dimensions	Unit, Location
Light green	40	3½"x 4½"	A6, B6
Medium green	40	3½" x 5¾"	A4, B4
Dark green	40	3½" x 7"	A2, B2
Light cream batik	24	2½" x 2½"	A7, B7
	24	2½" x 4"	A5, B5
	24	2½" x 5½"	A3, B3
	24	2½" x 7"	A1, B1
Medium blue batik	16	2½" x 2½"	A7, B7
	16	2½" x 4"	A5, B5
	16	2½" x 5½"	A3, B3
	16	2½" x 7"	A1, B1

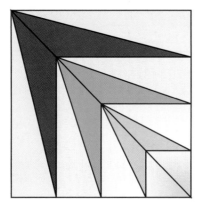

Fig. 2a.   *Make 8.*

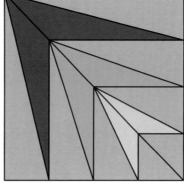

Fig. 2b.   *Make 4.*

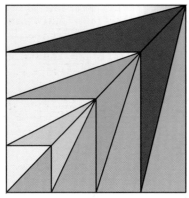

Fig. 2c.   *Make 4.*

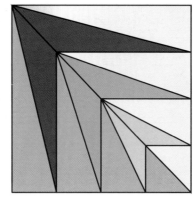

Fig. 2d.   *Make 4.*

Quilt Top Assembly

Arrange blocks as shown (Fig. 3). Sew blocks into horizontal rows and then join the rows.

Fig. 3.

Border Blocks and Binding

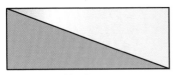

Rectangle block   **Square**

Cutting for borders and binding

Fabric	Cut pieces	Dimensions	Location
Light batik	4	6¾" x 19⅛"	All sides
Medium blue batik	4	6¾" x 19⅛"	All sides
Medium blue batik	4	6½" x 6½"	Corners
Medium blue batik	5	2" x 44"	Binding

(Make continuous binding as shown on pages 106–107.)

Cut 6¾" x 19⅛" rectangles in half as shown (Fig. 4).

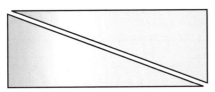 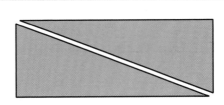

Fig. 4.

Before sewing, mark the ¼" seam allowances as shown and pin the pieces, matching seam allowances (Fig. 5).

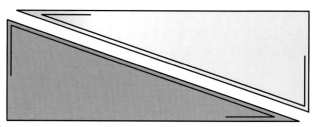

Fig. 5.

Sew the pieces together as illustrated (Fig. 6), offsetting the ends. Press the seams toward the dark side of the rectangle.

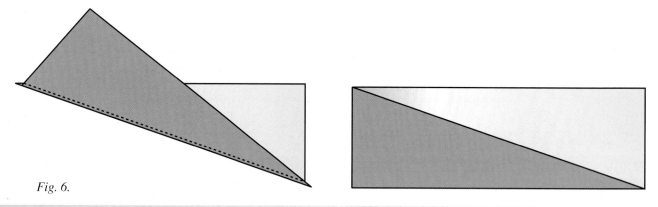

Fig. 6.

Combine border units as shown and sew borders onto quilt top as shown (Fig. 7).

Layer your quilt top with batting and backing; baste (refer to Finishing on page 105).

Fig. 7.

Quilting

The Palm blocks in SPIDER WEBS AND FAIRY FLOWERS were stipple quilted in the light batik areas with a zigzag design. Just for fun, Barbie Kanta quilted a spider web in the corners. After quilting, bind the edges and label your quilt.

SPIDER WEBS *Alternate Designs*

Change the look of your design by trying one of the alternate designs shown below (Fig. 8-10).

Fig. 8. Alternate design #1.

Fig. 9. Alternate design #2.

Fig. 10. Alternate design #3.

Palm

Unit A

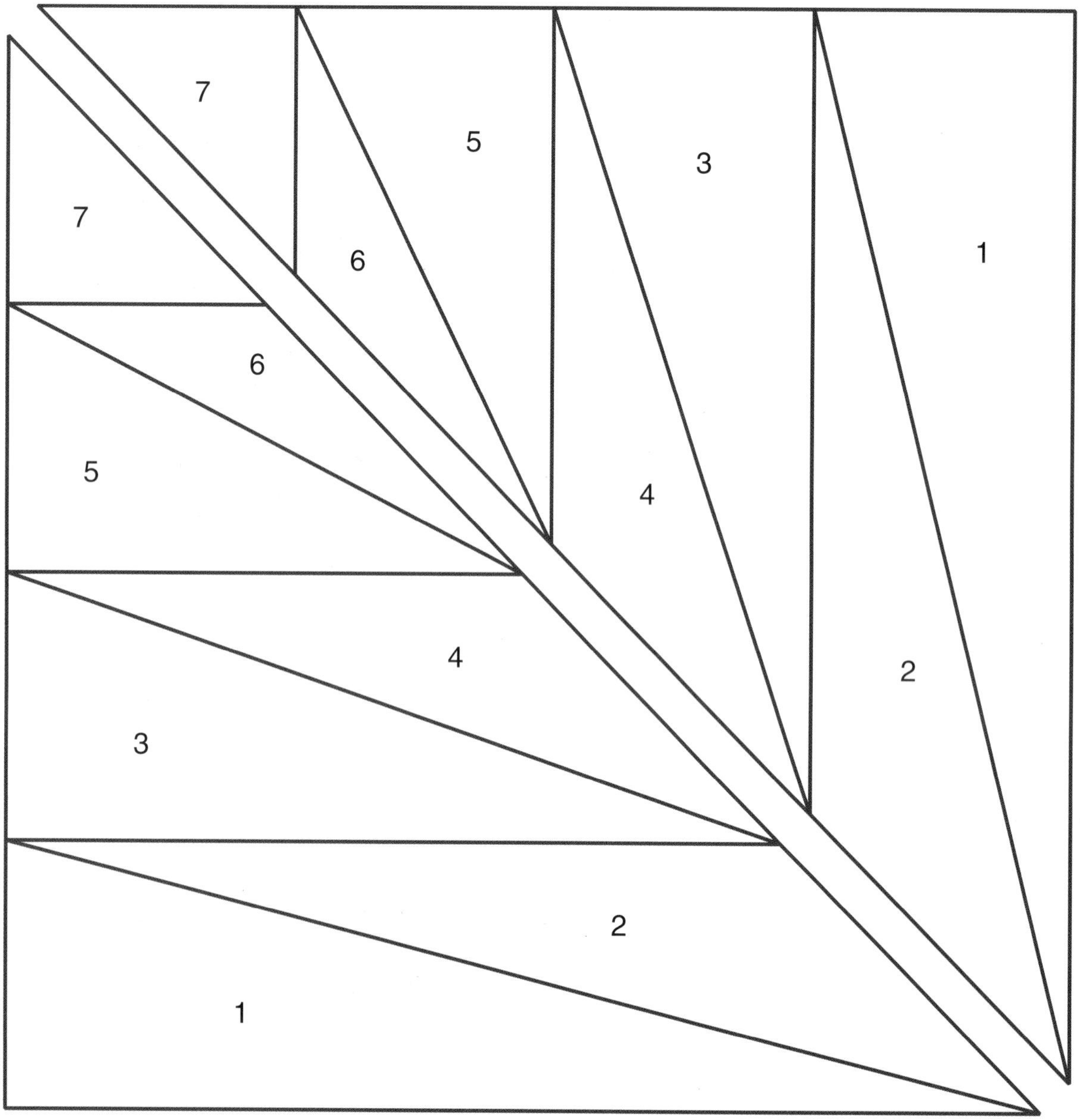

7

7

5

6

6

5

3

4

3

4

2

1

2

1

Unit B   Keep ¼" seam allowance outside units when trimming.

Rated
Intermediate

Sewing methods
Paper piecing
Traditional piecing

Quilt size
36" x 36"

Paper Pieced Blocks

Amaryllis

Pathway

Picket Fence

Plain Block

Plain

I must go seek some dewdrops here,
And hang a pearl in every cowslip's ear.

-William Shakespeare, "A Midsummer Night's Dream"

Cottage Garden

I'm fond of New England in general and of the Cape Cod area in particular. This charming quilt reminds me of gardens on Cape Cod and Martha's Vineyard. I was thrilled by the secondary star pattern in the center of the garden.

Fabrics

Blocks

White	¾ yard
Tan	¼ yard
Light blue	1¼ yards (includes binding)
Dark pink	¼ yard
Light pink	¼ yard
Dark green	¼ yard
Medium/dark green	¼ yard
Light green	⅜ yard
Grass green	¼ yard
Multicolored green	¼ yard (not a fat quarter)
Lavender	¼ yard

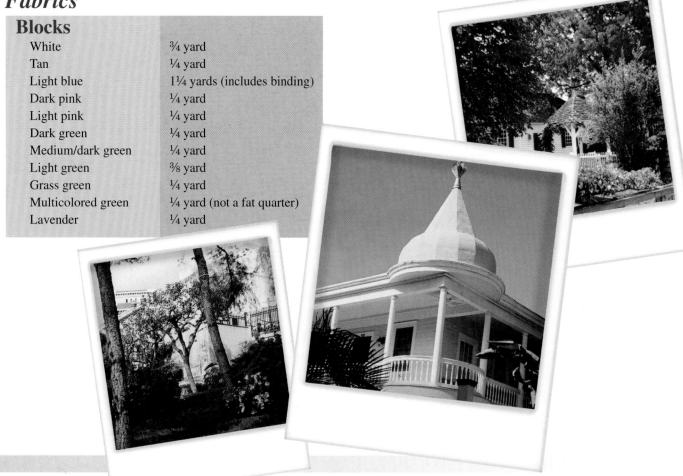

Plain
Make 4
Finished size: 6"

Cutting for Plain blocks

Fabric	Cut pieces	Dimensions	Location
Light blue	4	6½"	Border

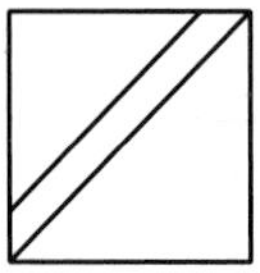

Pathway
Make 8
Finished size: 6"

Make eight paper copies of pattern on page 47. Cut out ½" beyond the outside lines.

Cutting for Pathway blocks ◹ *Cut square in half diagonally.*

Fabric	Cut pieces	Dimensions	Location
White	4	5¾" x 5¾" ◹	1
Dark green	8	2" x 10½"	2
Multicolored green	4	7¾" x 7¾" ◹	3

Make Pathway blocks as shown (Fig. 1). Trim to 6½".

Fig. 1.   Make 8.

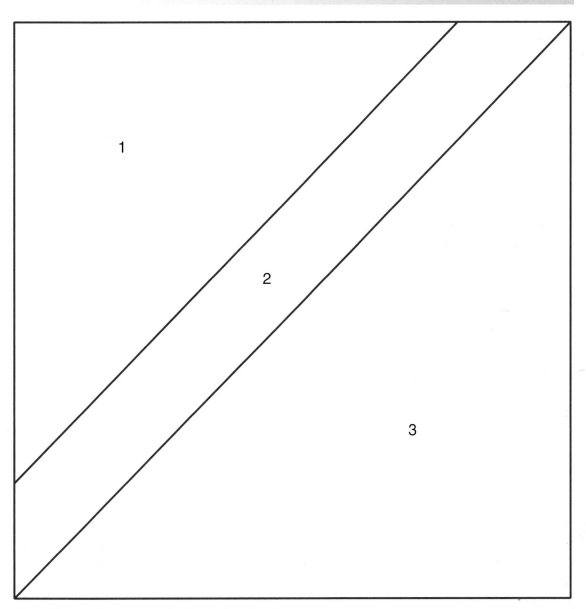

Pathway

Keep ¼" seam allowance outside block when trimming.

Amaryllis
Make 8
Finished size: 6"

Make eight paper copies of the six pattern units on page 52. Cut out ½" beyond the outside lines.

Make Amaryllis blocks, placing fabrics as shown (Fig. 2). Join Unit A to Unit B; add units C and D to either side of Unit AB. Add Unit E to Unit ABCD; and add Unit F to Unit ABCDE.

Cutting for Amaryllis blocks ◹ *Cut square in half diagonally.*

Fabric	Cut pieces	Dimensions	Unit, Location
Light blue	8	2¼" x 2¼"	A1
	8	2¾" x 2¾" ◹	A3, B3
	8	3" x 3" ◹	C2, D2
	16	2½" x 4"	E3, E5
Dark pink	8	2¾" x 2¾" ◹	A2, B2
	8	3" x 3" ◹	C1, D1
Light pink	8	2¼" x 2¼"	B1
	4	3½" x 3½" ◹	E1
Light green	16	2¾" x 4"	E2, E4
	4	4½" x 4½" ◹	F1
	8	3½" x 3½" ◹	F3, F5
Medium/dark green	4	4½" x 4½" ◹	F6
Lavender	8	3" x 3" ◹	F2, F4

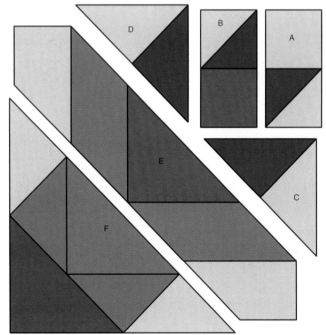

Fig. 2.

Make 8.

Picket Fence
Make 16*
Finished size: 6"

*See figure 3 for variations.

Make 24 paper copies of the Unit A and Unit B patterns on this page. Cut out ½" beyond the outside lines.

Sew 24 each of units A and B, then connect the units together to form eight of each Picket Fence block (Fig. 3).

Cutting for Picket Fence blocks

Fabric	Cut pieces	Dimensions	Location
White	24	2½" x 5"	A4
	24	3" x 3"	A1
Blue	48	2¾" x 2¾"	A2, A3
	48	3" x 3½"	B1, B3
Tan	48	1½" x 3"	B2, B4
Grass green	24	1¾" x 3"	B5

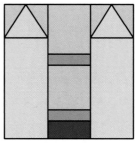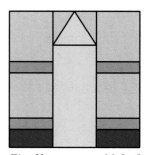

Fig. 3a.   Make 8.   Fig. 3b.   Make 8.

Picket Fence

Unit A

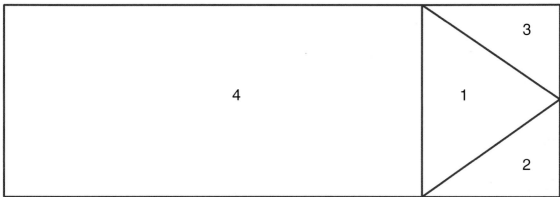

Keep ¼" seam allowance outside units when trimming.

Unit B

Quilt Top Assembly

Arrange blocks as shown (Fig. 4). Sew blocks into horizontal rows and then join the rows. Layer your quilt top with batting and backing; baste (refer to finishing, page 105).

Fig. 4.

Quilting

The flowers and picket fence in CottAGE GARDEN were outline quilted. The remainder of the quilt was stippled using light blue thread in the blue areas and white thread in the white areas. When the quilting is finished, bind the edges and make a label for your quilt.

Binding

Cutting for binding

Fabric	Cut pieces	Dimensions	Location
Light blue	4	2" x 38"	Binding
(Make continuous binding as shown on pages 106–107.)			

COTTAGE GARDEN *Alternate Designs*

Create a star design or a square within a square design by turning the Pathway blocks (Fig. 5 and 6).

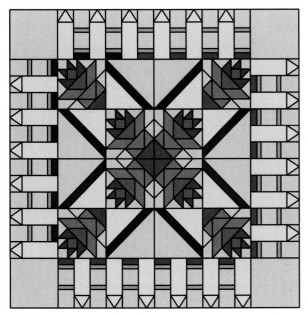

Fig. 5. Alternate design #1.

Fig. 6. Alternate design #2.

BUTTERFLIES IN MY GARDEN, 36" x 36", Ruth Spurlock, Columbia, Tennessee. Ruth created this beautiful quilt using numerous butterfly fabrics. The fabric in the picket fence gives a realistic look to this quilt.

Amaryllis

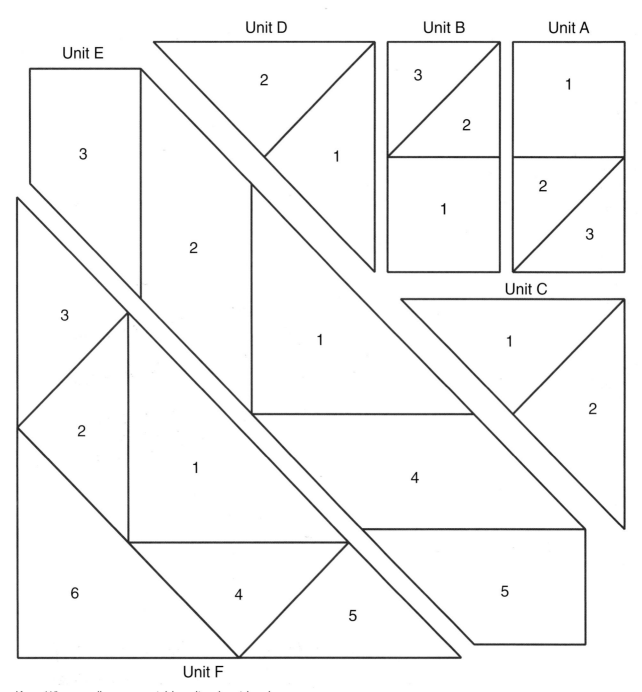

Keep ¼" seam allowance outside units when trimming.

Rated
Advanced

Sewing method
Paper piecing

Quilt size
48" x 48"

Paper Pieced Blocks

Split Star

Split

Snow Drop

Give me the splendid silent sun, with all his beams full-dazzling;
Give me juicy autumnal fruit, ripe and red from the orchard;
Give me a field where the unmow'd grass grows;
Give me an arbor, give me the trellis'd grape...
- Walt Whitman, "Give me the Splendid, Silent Sun"

Garden Trellis

An intricate design with the illusions of motion and depth, the trellis appears to float in front of the quilt. Use fall colors as shown or select bright summer colors for a different look.

Fabrics

Blocks and Border Blocks

White	2 yards
Tan	1½ yards
Dark tan	2 yards (Includes binding fabric)
Medium red	1½ yards
Dark red	¼ yard
Dark red	½ yard
Dark yellow	¼ yard
Dark green	1½ yards
Medium green	⅓ yard
Brown	⅓ yard

Split Star
Make 44*
Finished size: 6"

*See figure 2 for color variations.

Make 44 paper copies of pattern on page 57. Cut out ½" beyond the outside lines.

Make a total of 44 Split Star blocks in the eight variations shown below (Fig. 2).

Cutting for Split Star blocks

Fabric	Cut pieces	Dimensions	Location
Medium red	44	1½"x 9½"	A3
Dark green	88	3" x 7½"	A2, B2
White	24	3½" x 5½"	A4, B3
	24	4¼" x 7"	A1, B1
Tan	40	3½" x 5½"	A4, B3
	20	4¼" x 7"	A1, B1
Dark tan	24	3½" x 5½"	A4, B3
	24	4¼" x 7"	A1, B1

Fig. 2a. Make 8. *Fig. 2b.* Make 4. *Fig. 2c.* Make 4. *Fig. 2d.* Make 4.

Fig. 2e. Make 8. *Fig, 2f.* Make 8. *Fig. 2g.* Make 4. *Fig. 2h.* Make 4.

Split
Make 4
Finished size: 6"

Make four paper copies of the pattern below. Cut out ½" beyond the outside lines.

Cutting for Split blocks

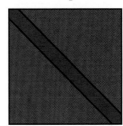

⬛ *Cut square in half diagonally.*

Fabric	Cut pieces	Dimensions	Location
Dark tan	4	7½" x 7½" ◨	2, 3
Medium red	4	1½" x 9½"	1

Make four Split blocks as shown (Fig. 1).

Fig. 1.   Make 4.

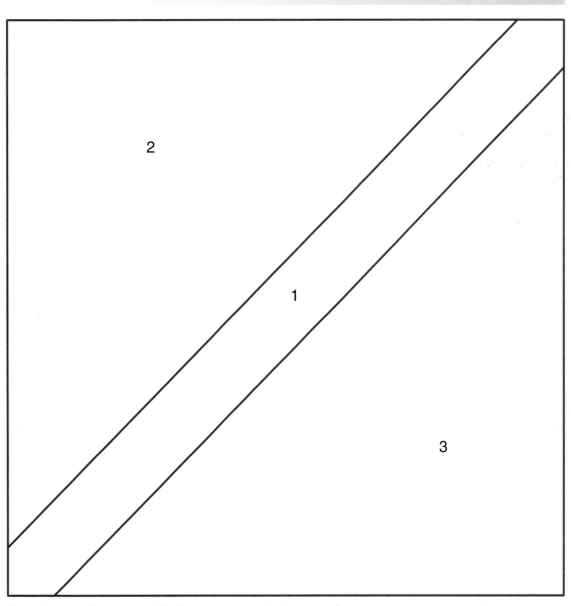

Split

2

1

3

Keep ¼" seam allowance outside block when trimming.

Snow Drop
Make 16*
Finished size: 6"

*See below for color variations.

Make 16 paper copies of the pattern on page 59. Cut out ½" beyond the outside lines.

Make 16 Snow Drop blocks placing fabrics as shown in the five variations of figure 3.

Cutting for Snow Drop blocks

⬛ *Cut square in half diagonally.*

Fabric	Cut pieces	Dimensions	Location
Dark yellow	16	1¼" x 1¼"	1
Medium red	16	2½" x 2½"	4
Dark red	16	3½" x 5"	5
Medium green	16	2½" x 4"	8
Dark green	16	2¾" x 5"	9
White	16	2½" x 2½"	2
	16	2" x 2½"	3
	16	2¾" x 4"	6
	16	2½" x 3¾"	7
	16	2½" x 5½"	10
	16	2½" x 5½"	11
	24	5" ⬛	12, 13, 14, 15
Brown	8	5" ⬛	12, 13, 14, 15

Fig. 3a.   Make 8.

Fig. 3b.   Make 2.

Fig. 3c.   Make 2.

Fig. 3d.   Make 2.   *Fig. 3e.   Make 2.*

Binding
Cutting for binding

Fabric	Cut pieces	Dimensions	Location
Dark tan	5	2" x 44"	Binding

(Make continuous binding as shown on pages 106–107.)

Split Star

Unit A

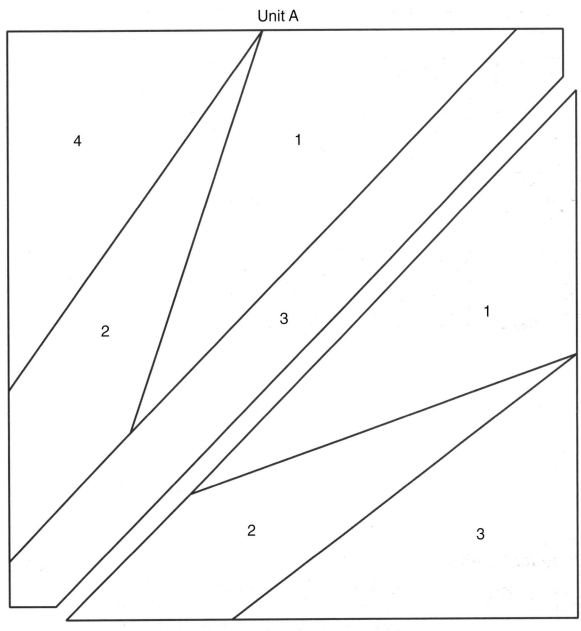

4

1

2

3

1

2

3

Unit B

Keep ¼" seam allowance outside units when trimming.

Quilt Top Assembly

Arrange the blocks as shown (Fig. 4). Sew blocks into horizontal rows and then join the rows.
Layer your quilt top with batting and backing; baste (refer to Finishing, page 105).

Fig. 4.

Quilting

GARDEN TRELLIS was stipple quilted in the light areas and outline quilted in the tan
and dark tan areas. After quilting, bind the edges and make a label for your quilt.

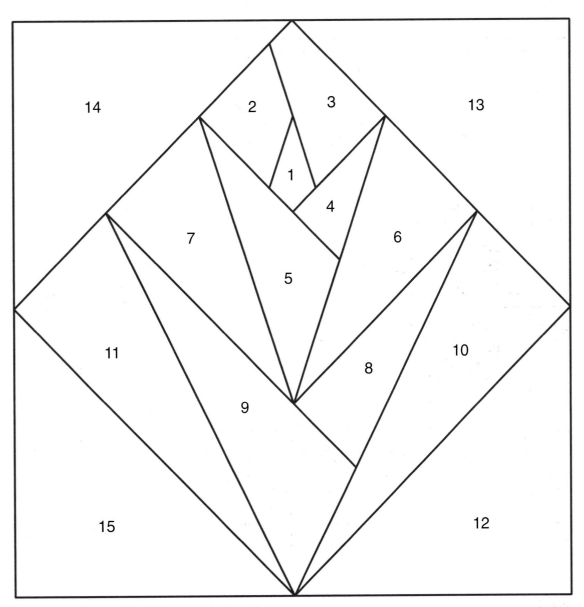

Keep ¼" seam allowance outside block when trimming.

I know a little garden-close
Set thick with lily and red rose,
Where I would wander if I might
From dewy dawn to dewy night,...
- William Morris, "The Nymph's Song to Hylas"

Spice of Life

As you select fabrics for this quilt, do not change the colors or values. They were chosen very carefully to create the illusion of transparency present in this quilt. But, if the illusion of transparency is not important to you, select any colors you wish. *Quilted by Barbie Kanta.*

Sewing method
Paper piecing

Quilt size
36" x 36"

Paper Pieced Blocks

Gentleman's Fancy

Crocus

Garden Maze

Garden Maze #2

Fabrics

Blocks and Border Blocks

Ivory	1½ yards
Dark green	⅓ yard
Medium green	½ yard
Dark orange	¼ yard
Medium orange	¼ yard
Medium dark red	½ yard
Dark red	¾ yard (includes binding)
Bright blue	⅓ yard
Tan	¼ yard
Dark tan	½ yard
Light blue	⅓ yard
Dark blue	½ yard

Gentleman's Fancy
Make 13
Finished size: 6"

Make 13 paper copies of the three pattern units on page 62. Cut out ½" beyond the outside lines.

Cutting for Gentleman's Fancy blocks

Fabric	Cut pieces	Dimensions	Location
Dark green	13	2¾"	A1
Ivory	52	2¾"	A2, A3, A4, A5
Medium green	52	3"	A6, A10, B1, C1
Bright blue	104	2¾"	A7, A8, C2, C3, A11, A12, B2, B3
Red	52	2¾"	B4, B5, C4, C5
Tan	52	3"	A9, A13, B6, C6

Make 13 Gentleman's Fancy blocks connecting Units A, B, and C as shown (Fig. 1).

Fig. 1.

Make 13.

Gentleman's Fancy

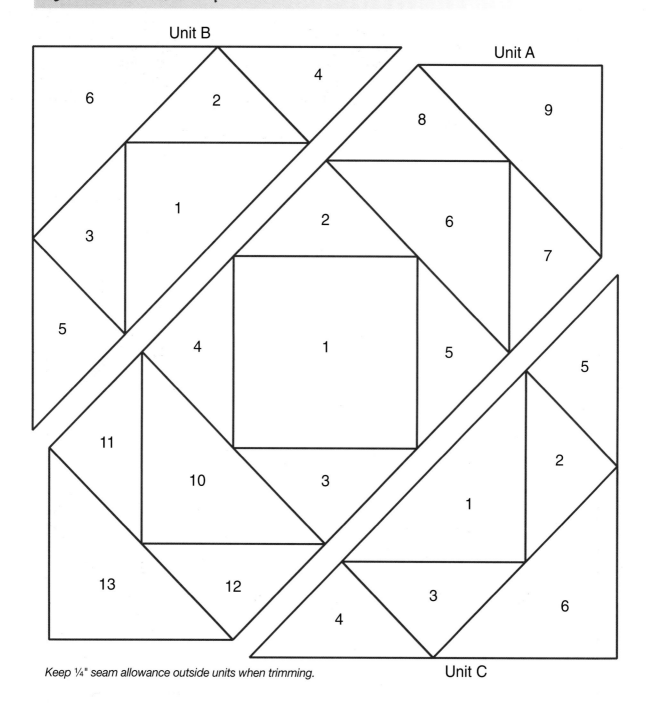

Keep ¼" seam allowance outside units when trimming.

Crocus
Make 12
Finished size: 6"

Make 12 paper copies of the pattern on this page. Cut out ½" beyond the outside lines.

Fig. 2 .   *Make 12.*

Cutting for Crocus blocks

Fabric	Cut pieces	Dimensions	Location
Ivory	12	2"	1
	24	2½" x 3¾"	4, 5
	24	2½" x 5¼"	8, 9
	48	3"	14, 15, 16, 17
Medium orange	12	1½" x 2"	2
Dark orange	12	2½" x 4"	3
Medium green	12	1¾" x 3½"	6
Dark green	12	2½" x 5½"	7
Medium dark red	48	1¼" x 5¼"	10, 11, 12, 13

Make 12 Crocus blocks as shown (Fig. 2).

Crocus

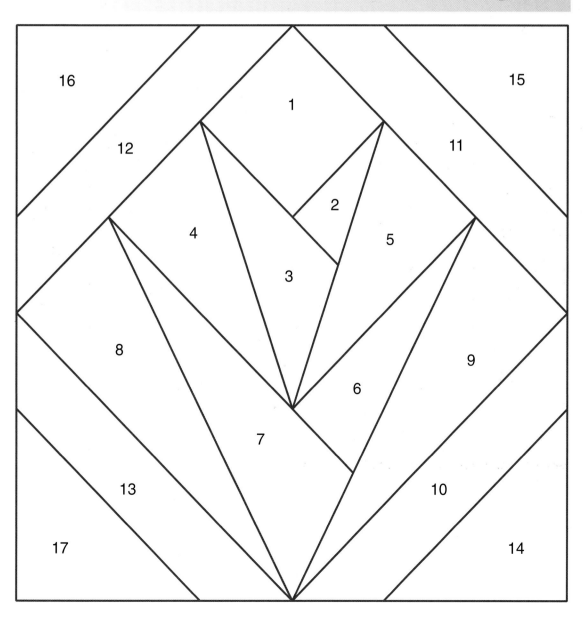

Quilt Top Assembly

Arrange blocks as shown (Fig. 3). Sew blocks into horizontal rows and then join the rows.

Fig. 3.

Border and Binding

Garden Maze
Make 20
Finished size: 3" x 6"

Make 20 paper copies of the three pattern units on this page.
Cut out ½" beyond the outside lines.

Make 20 Garden Maze blocks by connecting units A, B, and C as shown (Fig. 4).

Cutting for Garden Maze blocks and binding

Fabric	Cut pieces	Dimensions	Location
Light blue	20	2" x 3"	A1
Dark tan	40	1¼" x 3"	A2, A4
	40	2" x 2½"	A3, A5
Medium dark red	80	1¾" x 3¾"	A6, A8, B1, C1
Dark blue	40	1¾" x 3"	A7, B4
Dark red	40	2" x 2½"	B2, C3,
	40	1½" x 2¾"	C2, B3
	4	2" x 40"	Binding
(Make continuous binding as shown on pages 106–107.)			
Dark ivory	40	1¾" x 3"	A9, C4

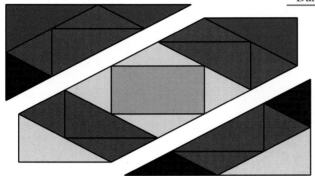

Fig. 4.

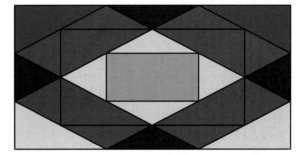

Make 20.

Garden Maze

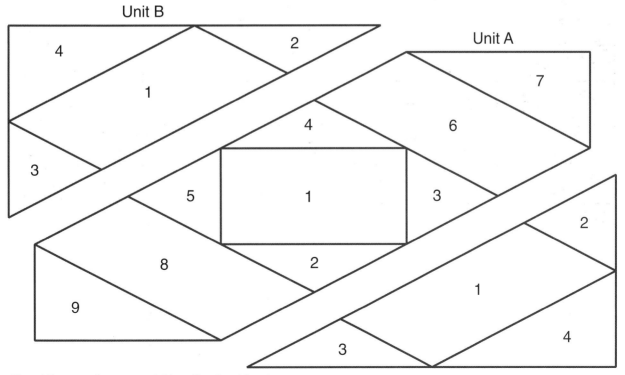

Keep ¼" seam allowance outside units when trimming.

Garden Maze #2
Make 4
Finished size: 3"

Make four paper copies of the three pattern units on this page. Cut out ½" beyond the outside lines.

Cutting for Garden Maze #2 block

Fabric	Cut pieces	Dimensions	Unit, Location
Light blue	4	2" x 2"	A1
Dark tan	16	1½" x 2¼"	A2, A3, A4, A5
Medium dark red	16	1½" x 2½"	A6, A8, B1, C1
Bright blue	12	2"	A7, A9, B4
Dark red	16	1½" x 1¾"	B2, B3, C2, C3
Dark ivory	4	1½" x 1¾"	C4

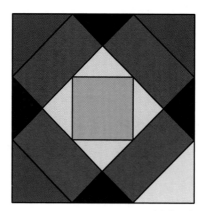

Fig. 5.

Make 4.

Make four Garden Maze #2 blocks by connecting the units as shown (Fig. 5).

Sew border blocks together as shown and add to the sides (Fig. 6, page 67). Repeat with the top and bottom borders.

Layer your quilt top with batting and backing; baste (refer to Finishing on page 105).

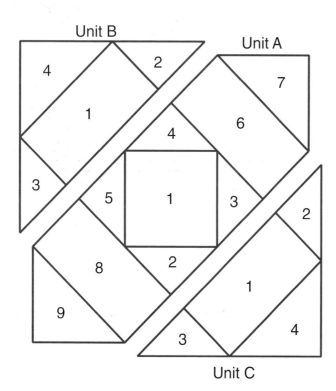

Unit B

Unit A

Unit C

Keep ¼" seam allowance outside units when trimming.

Fig. 6.

Quilting

The flowers and lattice in SPICE OF LIFE were outline quilted. If you prefer, stipple the light areas instead of outline quilting. After quilting, bind the edges and label your quilt.

"Summer afternoon–summer afternoon; to me those have always been the two most beautiful words in the English language."

- Henry James

Royal Palm

While visiting Thomas Edison's winter home in Fort Myers, Florida, I was surprised to learn there are many species of palms. This quilt, with its illusion of motion, was inspired by the majestic Royal Palm and numerous batik fabrics in my stash. Quilted by Barbie Kanta.

Rated
Advanced

Sewing method
Paper piecing

Quilt size
48" x 48"

Paper Pieced Blocks

Bluebell

Palm

Cactus Flower

Cactus Flower Variation

Fabrics

Background

Cream	2 yards
(Bluebell, Palm, and Cactus Flower blocks)	
Blue	2 yards
(Blocks, plus borders and binding)	

Bluebell Block

Four blue gradations*	#1	¼ yard
	#2	¼ yard
	#3	¼ yard
	#4	¼ yard
Dark green		¼ yard
Medium green		¼ yard

(*Rather than gradations of blue, you could use ¾ yard of a single blue fabric.)

Palm Block

Green	1 yard

Cactus Flower & Cactus Flower Variation

Dark green	¼ yard
Medium green	⅜ yard
Pink	⅜ yard
Light red	⅜ yard
Red	¼ yard
Dark red	⅜ yard

Bluebell
Make 4
Finished size: 6"

Make four paper copies of the pattern on page 70. Cut out ½" beyond the outside lines.

Fig. 1. Make 4.

Cutting for Bluebell blocks

Fabric	Cut pieces	Dimensions	Location
Cream	4	2¼" x 2¼"	1
	8	2" x 5"	4, 5
	8	2½" x 5½"	8, 9
	8	2¼" x 7"	12, 13
Light blue	4	1¾" x 2½"	2
Medium blue	4	2½" x 4½"	3
Dark blue	4	2" x 4"	6
Very dark blue	4	2½" x 5"	7
Light green	4	2½" x 5"	10
	4	2½" x 7"	11

Make four Bluebell blocks as shown (Fig. 1).

Bluebell

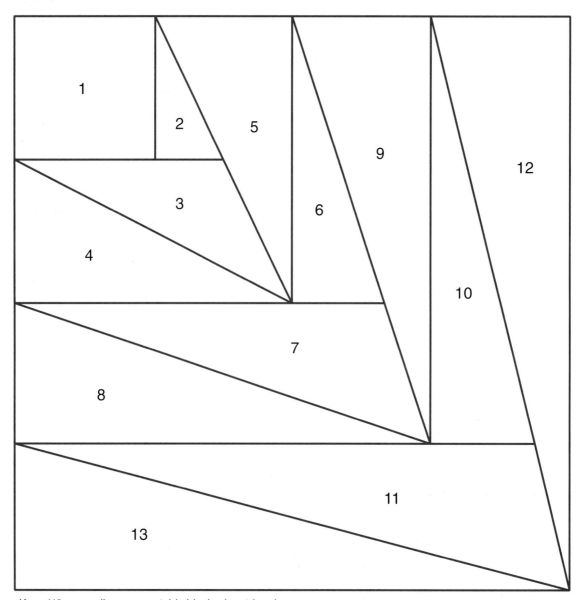

Keep ¼" seam allowance outside block when trimming.

Palm
Make 16*
Finished size: 6"

*See figure 2 for color variations.

Make 16 paper copies of both pattern units on page 73. Cut out ½" beyond the outside lines.

Make 16 Palm blocks as shown (Fig. 2), attaching Unit A to Unit B.

Cutting for Palm blocks

Fabric	Cut pieces	Dimensions	Unit, Location
Cream	16	2½" x 7"	#1 – A1
			#2 – B1
	16	2½" x 5½"	#1 – A3
			#2 – B3
	16	2½" x 4"	#1 – A5
			#2 – B5
	16	2½" x 2½"	#1 – A7
			#2 – B7
Green	32	2½" x 7"	#1 – A2, B2
			#2 – A2, B2
	32	2½" x 5½"	#1 – A4, B4
			#2 – A4, B4
	32	2½" x 4"	#1 – A6, B6
			#2 – A6, B6
Blue	16	2½" x 7"	#1 – B1
			#2 – A1
	16	2½" x 5½"	#1 – B3
			#2 – A3
	16	2½" x 4"	#1 – B5
			#2 – A5
	16	2½" x 2½"	#1 – B7
			#2 – A7

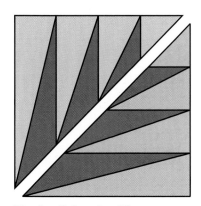

Fig. 2a. Coloration #1.

Make 8.

Fig. 2b. Coloration #2.

Make 8.

Palm

Unit A

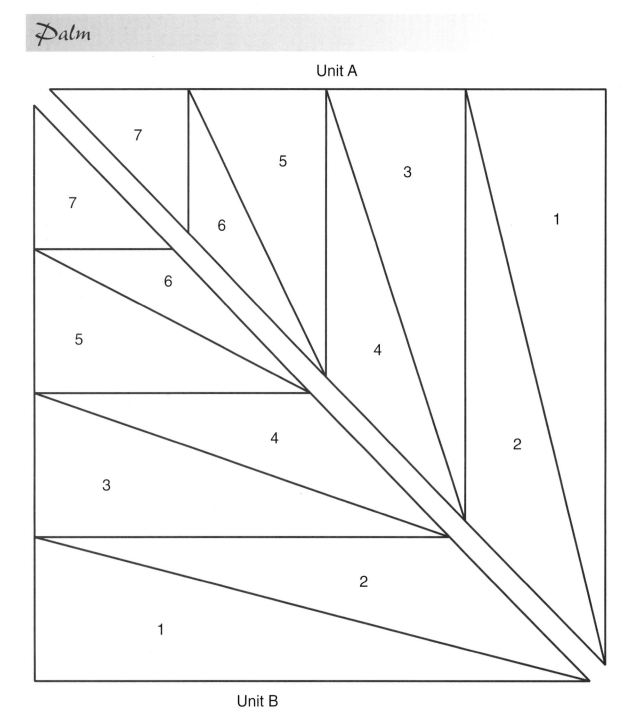

Unit B

Keep ¼" seam allowance outside units when trimming.

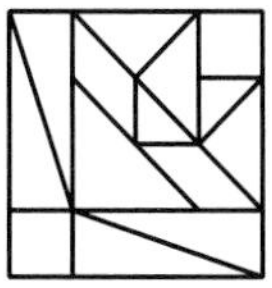

Cactus Flower
Make 16*
Finished size: 6"

*See below for color variations.

Make 16 paper copies of the four pattern units on page 74. Cut out ½" beyond the outside lines.

Make 16 Cactus Flower blocks as shown (Fig. 3), attaching Units A, B, C, and D to form the block.

Cutting for Cactus Flower blocks

Fabric	Cut pieces	Dimensions	Unit, Location
Cream	12	2¼" x 2¼"	#1 – A1
	24	3" x 4"	#1 – A3, A5
	24	2¼" x 5¾"	#1 – C2, D1
Blue	4	2¼" x 2¼"	#2 – A1
	8	3" x 4"	#2 – A3, A5
	8	2¼" x 5¾"	#2 – C2, D1
Pink	16	2¾" x 2¾"	#1 – A2
			#2 – A2
Light red	16	2½" x 4"	#1 – A4
			#2 – A4
	16	2½" x 2½"	#1 – B2
			#2 – B2
Red	32	2½" x 3½"	#1 – B1, B3
			#2 – B1, B3
Dark red	16	4" x 4"	#1 – B4
			#2 – B4
Light green	32	2¼" x 5¾"	#1 – C1, D2
			#2 – C1, D2
Dark green	16	2¼" x 2¼"	#1 – C3
			#2 – C3

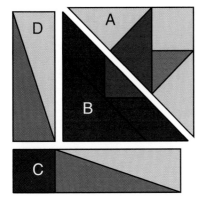

Fig. 3a. Coloration #1.

Make 12 blocks.

Fig. 3b. Coloration #2.

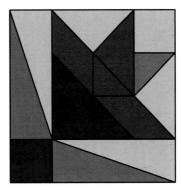

Make 4 blocks.

Cactus Flower

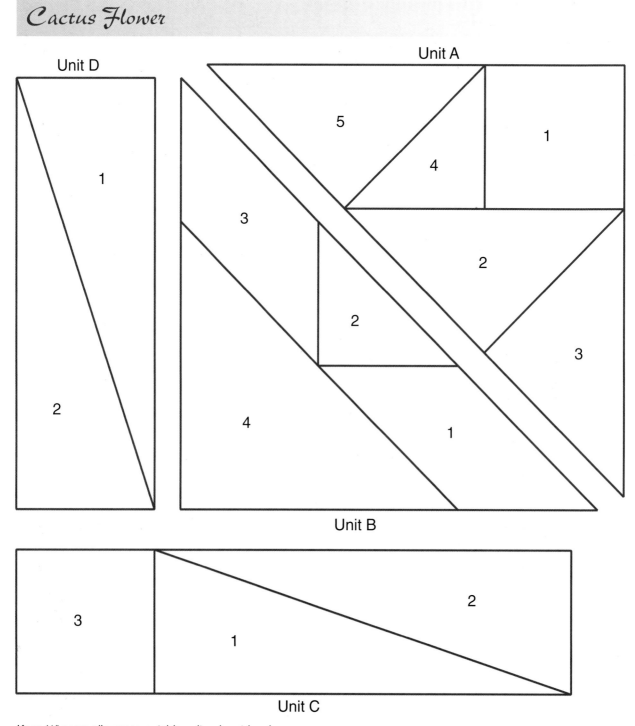

Keep ¼" seam allowance outside units when trimming.

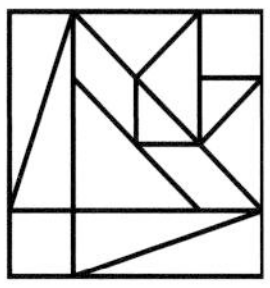

Cactus Flower Variation
Make 12
Finished size: 6"

Make 12 paper copies of the four pattern units on page 78. Cut out ½" beyond the outside lines.

Make 12 Cactus Flower Variation blocks as shown (Fig. 4), attaching Units A, B, C, and D to form the block.

Cutting for Cactus Flower Variation blocks

Fabric	Cut pieces	Dimensions	Location
Cream	12	2¼" x 2¼"	A1
	24	3" x 4"	A3, A5
	24	2¼" x 5¾"	C3, D1
Pink	12	2¾" x 2¾"	A2
Light red	12	2½" x 4"	A4
	12	2½" x 2½"	B2
Red	24	2½" x 3½"	B1, B3
Dark red	12	4" x 4"	B4
Light green	24	2¼" x 5¾"	C2, D2
Dark green	12	2¼" x 2¼"	C1

Fig. 4.

Make 12.

Quilt Top Assembly

Arrange blocks as shown (Fig. 5). Sew the blocks into horizontal rows and then join the rows.

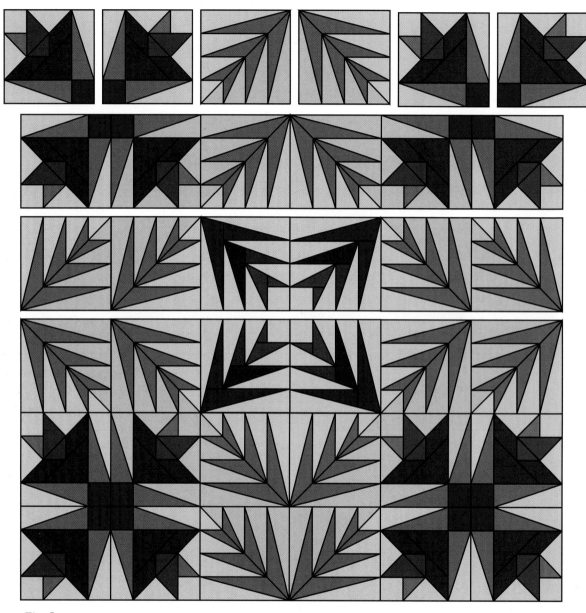

Fig. 5.

Borders and Binding

Cutting for borders and binding

Fabric	Cut pieces	Dimensions	Location
Gold	4	3½" x 24½"	Top, bottom and side borders
Dark blue	4	3½" x 24½"	Top, bottom and side borders
Dark blue	5	2" x 44"	Binding
		(Make continuous binding as shown on pages 106–107.)	

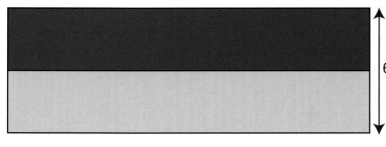

6½"

Fig. 6. Strip should measure 6½"

Sew strips of gold and dark blue fabric together to form the border (Fig. 6). This strip should measure 6½" wide after it is sewn. Press seams toward the darker strip.

Sew a Cactus block onto each end of two border strips as shown. Press the seams open. Then sew the strips onto the sides of the quilt (Fig. 7) and press the seams away from the quilt.

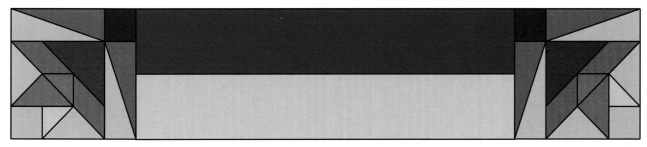

Fig. 7.

Fig. 8.

Sew two Cactus blocks onto each end of the two remaining border strips as shown (Fig. 8). Press the seams open. Sew the strips onto the top and bottom of the quilt and press the seams away from the quilt.

Layer your quilt top with batting and backing; baste (refer to Finishing on page 105).

Cactus Flower Variation

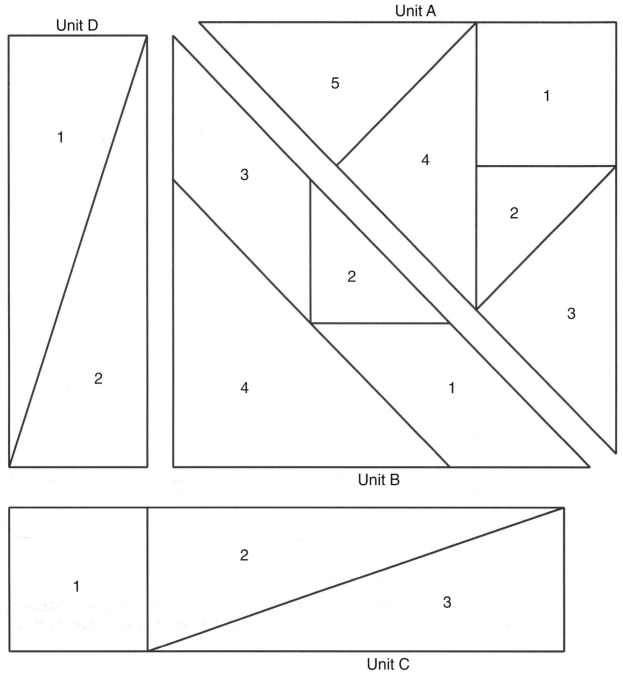

Unit D

Unit A

Unit B

Unit C

Keep ¼" seam allowance outside units when trimming.

Quilting

Longarm machine quilter, Barbie Kanta, outline quilted the flower shapes, the leaves in the borders, and the zigzags in the medium blue area. Another option would be to stipple quilt the yellow and blue areas which will serve to puff out the flower and palm blocks. After quilting, bind the edges and make a label for your quilt.

ROYAL PALM *Alternate Designs*

ROYAL ILLUSION, 52" x 52". This beautiful Royal Palm variation was created by Scottie Pendleton of Antioch, California.

ROYAL PALM, 60" x 60". Roberta McIntire of Walnut Creek, California, created this intriguing Royal Palm variation.

"Art is unquestionably one of the purest and highest elements in human happiness. It trains the mind through the eye, and the eye through the mind. As the sun colors flowers, so does art color life."

- John Lubbock

Fabric Suggestions

Selecting fabric for a quilt can be difficult. At times, it can feel downright impossible. Color is not the only consideration when selecting fabric for a quilt. While it is important, texture and value are equally important. Often, when a quilter is having trouble selecting fabric for a quilt, the color may not be the trouble; instead it may be the value or the texture of the fabrics.

When selecting fabric for your quilt, be sure to consider color, texture, and value as you make your choices.

Texture

Very simply, texture is the pattern of the fabric. Visual texture can also be regarded as the movement in the pattern of the fabric. A busy print has much visual texture or movement (Fig. 1), while a non-busy print has little visual texture or movement (Fig. 2). A solid fabric has no visual texture (Fig. 3).

Non-busy fabrics appear to be solid, but still have a slight visual texture or print to them. These fabrics are said to read like a solid fabric even though they have a texture. You should consider using some of these types of fabrics in your quilt. While these types of fabrics may not be the most exciting ones on the bolt at the fabric store, they will add visual interest to your quilt without overwhelming the eye with texture.

When selecting fabrics for your quilt, you'll need both busy and non-busy prints. If all the prints in your quilt are busy, the prints will distract from the block design, overwhelm the eye, and the design may be lost. Notice the block below which contains too many busy prints (Fig. 4). In fact, the fabrics are so busy they almost obliterate the block design.

If all the fabrics in your quilt are solid, the blocks will be boring (Fig. 5). While the design is easy to see, a block with little visual texture is rather uninteresting.

When there is a good balance between busy and non-busy prints, the block is interesting and pleasing (Fig. 6).

Fig. 1. Busy prints (much texture).

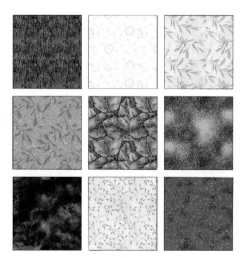

Fig. 2. Non-busy prints (little texture).

Fig. 4. There are too many busy prints in this block.

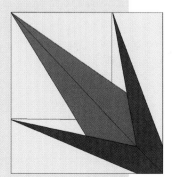

Fig. 5. With all solid fabrics, this block is too plain.

Fig. 6. Nice balance of busy and non-busy prints.

Fig. 3. Solid fabrics (no texture).

Value

Value is another consideration when selecting fabric for your quilt. Your quilt should have light, medium, and dark value fabrics. What is value? Value is the lightness and darkness of a fabric, not how much you pay for it at the store!

The following examples will help you understand how to achieve the right balance of light and dark in your quilts.

Without the right mix of lights, mediums, and darks, a quilt will lack sparkle and may look flat. The colors may be right, the textures may be perfect, but if a quilt contains only one value, the quilt will not "shine" as it should (Fig. 7).

On the other hand, if block contains medium, light, and dark values, it will be interesting (Fig. 8).

At first it may be hard to determine whether a fabric is of light value, medium value, or dark value. There are several ways to determine the fabric's value.

The Squint Test

After laying out several fabrics, squint at the fabrics. Squinting blurs your vision and this may help you determine if you have a light, medium, or dark fabric.

If the fabrics look much the same (Fig. 9), there is not enough difference in their values. You need to see a definite light, a definite medium, and a definite dark in your fabric selection.

Using a Value Tool

If squinting does not help you determine value, you can use a tool called a value finder that will help. You can buy value finder tools at your local quilt store or you can make your own.

Value finder tools will work on busy, multicolored prints as well as non-busy prints. To use on multicolored fabrics, overlap the value finders and look through both of them. When the tools are overlapped, they will work on most fabrics, no matter what their colors.

To use the value finders, place them close to your eyes and look through them. When you look through a value finder, you will find that the color of the fabric is gone and only the lightness or darkness of the fabric is seen. This invaluable tool allows you to easily check the values and make sure you have light, medium, and dark values in your fabrics.

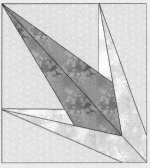

Fig. 7. While the quilt block has a nice misty quality, the values are too similar; there are no mediums and darks to give the block interest.

Fig. 8. Adding medium and dark fabrics to the block gives a pleasing look and the quilt will have sparkle.

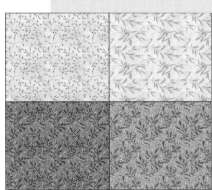

Fig. 9. These fabrics are all light and medium-light fabrics.

Make your own value finder

Purchase two transparent report covers of the kind with clip-on spines. These are available at office supply and discount stores. Select a red report cover and a green report cover. Cut out a piece at least 3" x 5" from each cover. Voilá! You have just made your own value finder. Of course, you can make them larger than 3" x 5" if you wish.

You will need both a red value finder and a green value finder. A red value finder does not work on red fabrics, so you will need to use the green one when viewing reds. Also, the green value tool does not work on green fabrics, so you need to use the red one when viewing greens.

The fabrics in figure 10 shade from light to dark. This is a good example of light, medium, and dark fabrics. When these fabrics are viewed through the value tool, they will look like the value line in figure 11:

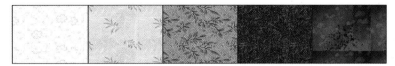

Fig. 10. Fabric shading from light to dark.

Fig. 11. Value line shading from light to dark.

Gradated fabrics

Several of the quilts in this book use gradated fabrics sets (Fig. 12). These fabrics generate a luminous glow in quilts. A gradated fabric set is fabric of a single color; however, it varies from light to dark. You can find these types of fabrics in packets of hand-dyed fabric, or in commercial prints (Fig. 13).

Fig. 12. Blue fabric gradated eight steps, from light to dark values.

Fig. 13. Examples of gradated commercial and hand–dyed fabrics.

Color

There are several ways to select colors for a quilt. You can make a quilt to match the colors in a room, you can use your favorite colors, or you can be inspired by a color combination you have seen in nature.

Photographs can also inspire a color combination. The quilt GARDEN TRELLIS (page 53) was inspired by a photograph of a garden in Historic Williamsburg, Virginia.

Wallpaper, upholstery fabric, or even pottery can provide inspiration for color combinations. The plate in figure 14 was made in India. Its soft blues and greens inspired TEAR DROPS, the quilt on page 23.

A fabric can also inspire the entire color scheme for a quilt. In the quilt STAR GLOW (page 33), the multicolored fabric used in the border was selected first. If you look closely at the fabric, you will see it has red, green, cream, and gold in the fabric print.

Using the border fabric as a guide, medium gold, cream, dark, medium and light green, and dark and medium red were selected as the colors for this quilt (Fig. 15).

When selecting fabrics for quilts, consider not only the color, but also the value and texture. Make sure to select light, medium, and dark values as well as non-busy and busy prints. This will produce a quilt design that sparkles.

Fig. 14. The plate in the photo was the inspiration for the fabric combination in the quilt TEAR DROPS.

Illusions

While not exclusively related to color, there are two other considerations in fabric selection and placement. They are transparency and motion, and as they relate to quilting, both are illusions.

Transparency

If something is transparent, it allows light to pass through so that objects on the other side can be clearly seen. The illusion of transparency is an illusion of layers, of something transparent being laid over or under something else.

In the quilt SPICE OF LIFE (page 60), the illusion of transparency is seen within the lattice. It appears that the lattice is in the foreground, over the Gentleman's Fancy blocks.

Fig. 15. Fabrics in STAR GLOW *were selected from colors in the border fabric.*

Motion

When there is no actual motion, this refers to an implied motion – the arrangement of the parts of an image to create a sense of movement by using lines, shapes, forms, and textures that cause the eye to move over the work, thus producing the illusion of motion.

Motion can be created in several ways, by repeating a figure or shape as seen in RING AROUND THE POSY (page 9) or ROYAL PALM (page 68).

It can also be created by the use of diagonal lines. Quilts filled with diagonal lines tend to look very dramatic. This can be seen in the quilts SPIDER WEBS AND FAIRY FLOWERS (page 38), GARDEN TRELLIS (page 53), and ROYAL PALM (page 68).

"Live in each season as it passes, breathe the air, drink the drink, taste the fruit, and resign yourself to the influences of each."

- Henry David Thoreau

Fabric Cutting

Cutting Tools

Rotary Cutters

Rotary cutters have made quiltmaking fast and very accurate. Rotary cutters must be used with thick acrylic or plastic rulers called rotary rulers. With these tools it is possible to cut many layers of fabric at one time. You can cut squares, rectangles, triangles, and other shapes with amazing accuracy and lightning speed!

A rotary cutter resembles a pizza cutter, but it is much sharper. The cutter has a built-in guard to shield the sharp blade when not in use. Always close the guard when the cutter is not in use. Stand up when rotary cutting; you will have a better view and will have more control over the ruler and cutter.

Safety Tips

Make sure to close the guard whenever the rotary cutter is not in use.

Keep fingers away from the unprotected blade.

Keep rotary cutters out of the reach of children.

Cut away from yourself, never toward yourself.

Carefully clean or replace blades as soon as they begin to show wear. Worn blades tend to skip along the fabric instead of cutting smoothly and cleanly.

Rotary Mat

You will need to use a self-healing cutting mat with your rotary cutter and rotary ruler. A self-healing mat seals blade cuts and will last for several years. The mat protects your work surface from the sharp blade and makes your blades last longer. If you use a rotary cutter without a cutting mat, the blade will dull almost instantly.

If you have a large cutting area to work on, a 24" x 36" mat is a good size to have. If you don't have a large cutting area, you might consider an 18" x 24" mat which is the size most quilters use.

Be sure to store your mat flat; do not fold it. Keep it away from direct sunlight and heat as they can warp the mat. If you have room, keep your mat in your sewing room, flat on a table. That way you will always have a handy cutting surface.

Many quilters don't have the luxury of a sewing room, so they need to store their quilting supplies when not in use. There are several ways to store your mat. You can put it flat against a wall, possibly behind a sofa or a bookcase where it will remain flat and not warp.

You can also store a mat by hanging it. Clip it to a skirt hanger with soft protectors on the clips. The protectors will prevent the sharp clips from scratching the mat's soft surface.

Rotary Rulers

There are many types of rotary rulers. The most useful rulers are made of heavy, clear plastic or acrylic and are ⅛" thick with straight, smooth edges (Fig. 16). Many quilters favor 6" x 24" or 6" x 12" rulers for cutting strips, and 6" x 6" rulers for cutting squares and triangles. To have maximum usefulness, rulers should be marked with ⅛" increments. You may find that lip features on a ruler make them harder to use.

You can find rulers with yellow markings, black markings, and even pink markings. Try out different brands to see which works best for you.

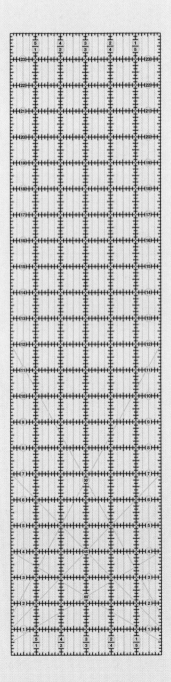

Fig. 16. A ruler made especially for use with rotary cutters.

Preshrinking and Checking Fabric for Colorfastness

Sort your fabrics into light and dark piles, unfolding them to a single layer as you sort.

Place the fabrics into your washer and let them set in warm, clear water. Do not use detergent. Check periodically to see if the water is clear. If it is not clear, the fabric is bleeding and the dyes will need to be set before the fabric is used.

If the fabric is colorfast, spin the water out and place the fabrics in your dryer. Tumble dry until the fabrics are slightly damp, then iron them, using a light spray sizing.

Setting Fabric Dyes

If you have a fabric that bleeds, this may help set the dye.

Immerse the fabric into undiluted white vinegar. One quart of white vinegar will set approximately 1½ yards of fabric.

Let the fabric set for a few minutes, then rinse thoroughly in clear, warm water. Repeat the colorfast test described above.

If the fabric does not bleed, dry the fabric until slightly damp and iron, using a light spray sizing. But, if the fabric still bleeds, do not use it in your quilt. Instead, find another fabric to use in its place. Most fabrics don't bleed; the most likely colors to do so are deep, rich colors, reds, and purples.

Instead of vinegar you can also use a product called Retayne™, which is a dye fixative for commercially dyed fabrics.

Rotary Cutting Techniques

Rotary Cutting Strips

Cotton fabric varies in width. In order to buy enough fabric, assume the width of the fabric is 42" to 44", no matter what it says on the end of the bolt!

Unless specifically noted otherwise, fabrics are cut on the crosswise grain, from selvage to selvage.

The following instructions are for right-handed quilters. If you are left-handed, reverse the instructions and use a ruler with markings both for right- and left-handed quilters.

1. Place fabric on the cutting mat and fold it in half. The fold of the fabric should be closest to you. Make sure the fabric is not wrinkled. If your rotary blade is sharp, you can stack several layers of fabric, but stack no more than three or four fabrics which will give you six or eight layers.

   The fold of the top fabric should be ¼" or so above the fold of the fabric below. This ensures that your strips will be cut at 90-degree angles to the fold.

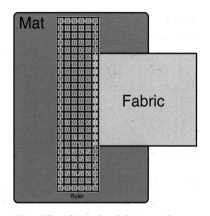

Fig. 17. Align the fabric and your rotary ruler over a vertical line on the rotary mat.

2. Align the bottom fabric with a horizontal line on your cutting mat. Move the left vertical edge of the fabric until it is slightly over a vertical line on your cutting mat (Fig. 17).

3. Trim the edge of the fabric by placing a 6" x 12" or 6" x 24" rotary ruler on the vertical line of the cutting mat.

   Place the weight of your left hand on the ruler; keep one finger along the left edge of the ruler to prevent it from slipping. With your right hand, open the cutter guard and hold the cutter straight, with the blade snugly against the right edge of the ruler.

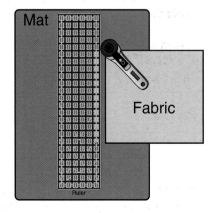

Fig. 18. As described above, roll the cutter along the right edge of the ruler, maintaining an even pressure.

Firmly press down on the cutter and push it away from you in a smooth, strong motion, maintaining a uniform firm pressure (Fig. 18). Keep the blade tight against the ruler and do not make short jerky cuts.

4. Remove the trimmed edges of fabric from the mat. These can be thrown away. Slide the ruler over to the right, until the markings on the ruler are at the desired strip width. For example, if you wish to cut 3½" strips, align the left edge of your fabric exactly with the 3½" markings on the ruler.

5. Cut as many strips in the desired size as you need. Replace the guard on the rotary cutter before setting it down.

Cutting Shapes from Strips

Once you have cut strips, you can cut different shapes from them. Squares, triangles, and rectangles can be quickly cut from strips (Fig. 19). Check each pattern to determine the size and shape you need to cut.

Squares: To rotary cut a square, cut a strip the desired depth of your square by the width of the fabric. Usually the width will be 44"; however, your fabric width may vary slightly.

Lay a strip on the cutting mat and place a 6" x 6" ruler on the strip. Trim the left edge, if needed. Move the ruler over until the desired measurement for your square is even with the left edge of the fabric. Cut the squares (Fig. 20).

Triangles: To rotary cut triangles from squares, cut a strip the measurement listed in your project by the width of the fabric.

Lay the strip on a cutting mat and place a 6" x 6" ruler over it. Remove the selvages and trim the left edge even. Move the ruler over until the desired measurement marking is even with the left edge of the fabric. Cut squares first and then cut the squares from corner to corner (Fig. 21).

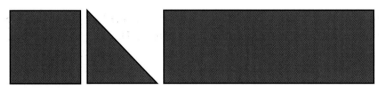

Fig. 19. Square, half-square triangle, and rectangle shapes cut from a strip.

Fig. 20. Cut squares from a pre-cut strip.

Fig. 21. To cut triangles from squares, first cut strips across the width of the fabric, then cut squares, and finally cut the squares from corner to corner.

Rectangles: To rotary cut rectangles, cut a strip the width of the fabric by the narrowest measurement of your rectangle.

Lay the strip on a cutting mat and place a 6" x 6" or 9" x 9" ruler on the strip. Trim off the selvages and even the left edge. Move the ruler over until the longest of the two rectangle measurements is even with the left edge of the fabric. Cut the rectangles (Fig. 22).

Fig. 22. Rectangle cut from pre-cut strip.

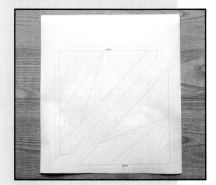

Fig. 23.

Templates

Some quilters prefer to use templates rather than paper piece. The following method, using freezer paper, allows you to make templates from the paper piecing patterns. To make templates, follow steps 1–4:

1. Photocopy the pattern you wish to make from the project you have chosen (Fig. 23). Cut out ½" beyond the outside lines.

2. Trace each piece of the pattern onto the dull side of freezer paper, making as many of each as needed (Fig. 24). For example, if you need eight of Template #1, trace #1 eight times. Do not add seam allowances. Mark the grain line on the freezer paper if you wish.

3. Cut the freezer paper patches apart to use as templates and iron each template onto the wrong side of the fabric (Fig. 25).

4. Using a rotary cutter, mat, and rotary ruler, cut out the fabric patches (Fig. 26) adding a ¼" seam allowance as you cut (Fig. 27).

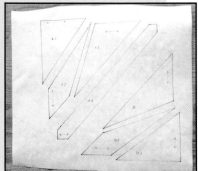

Fig. 24.

Fig. 25.

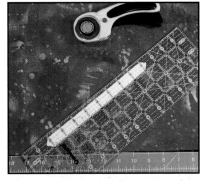

Fig. 26.

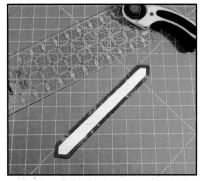

Fig. 27.

*Many eyes go through the meadow,
but few see the flowers in it.*
- Ralph Waldo Emerson, Journals, 1834

Paper Piecing

If you have never paper pieced before, take the time to review the supplies listed in this section. In addition, I strongly recommend that you do the mini-lesson on pages 92-96 that takes you through making a label for a quilt using paper piecing techniques. It may seem odd to make a label before you have made a quilt, but it's a good way to learn this paper piecing technique.

Tools & Supplies

Sewing machine – recently cleaned, tuned up, and threaded with off-white thread.

Open toe foot – a special presser foot for your sewing machine that will give better visibility when paper piecing.

Sewing machine needles – For paper piecing, use a size 90/14 needle. This needle is larger and creates a larger hole in the paper foundation, which in turn makes the paper easier to remove.

Iron – use to press (not iron) without steam.

6" and 12" Add-A-Quarter™ rulers – for trimming fabric while paper piecing. If you can't find this ruler at your local quilt store, you can make one from a 1" x 6" rotary ruler (Fig. 28). Just add ¼" masking tape strips along one edge until a "lip" has been built up.

Postcard or heavy index card – You will fold the paper foundation against this card before trimming it with an Add-A-Quarter ruler.

Rotary cutter and mat

Rotary rulers – sizes 6" x 6", 6" x 12", 9" x 9", 6" x 24"

Sandpaper grips – Attach these to the edges of your rotary ruler or postcard if they tend to slip as you use them.

Flowerhead pins and/or glue stick

Wooden iron – small, hand-held, wooden pressing tool.

A pad of small, stick-on notes – for labeling fabric pieces with placement numbers.

Transparent removable tape – for repairing torn paper foundations.

Copy paper – for making photocopies of paper piecing patterns. You can also use a lightweight paper such as doodle paper by Crayola®.

Fabric – 100% cotton. Use the best quality fabric you can find.

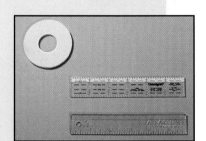

Fig. 28. Making a ruler with a lip, similar to an Add-A-Quarter ruler.

Paper Piecing Hints

Paper Removal

Tearing the paper off the back of the blocks when the quilt is finished can be difficult. However, using these sewing hints will make it a snap.

• Sewing machine needle – While paper piecing, use a 90/14 universal needle. This will leave a larger hole in the paper and make it easier to tear off.

- Stitch length – Set your straight stitch length to 1.5, or 18-20 stitches to the inch. This also aids in tearing the paper off because it adds extra perforations to the paper.

Tear the paper off when the quilt is finished. This is a mindless activity that can be done while watching a favorite TV program or talking on the phone to a friend. It's a treat to sit, watch TV, and work on the quilt, knowing the top is finished.

More Helpful Hints

- Thread – Thread your sewing machine with light gray or off-white thread. These neutral colors will work with any color fabric.

- Ironing station – Cover your ironing board with a piece of muslin to protect it from the possibility of ink from the paper foundation rubbing off onto your ironing board.

- Iron – Set your iron on a high setting with no steam. In fact, dump any water out of the iron. In paper piecing, using steam can warp the paper and cause distortion in your pattern. Once the quilt is finished and the paper removed, this guideline changes. With the paper gone, an iron with steam can be used to press the quilt top.

Paper Piecing Techniques
Making a ROYAL PALM Quilt Label (Fig. 29)

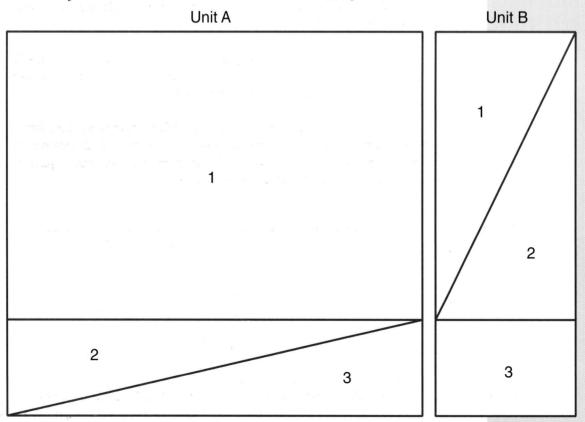

Unit A   Unit B

Keep ¼" seam allowance outside units when trimming.

Fig. 29.

Fabrics

(Since this label requires very little fabric, use pieces you have on hand.)

Tan or white-on-white fabric

Dark green

Medium green

Some quilters don't know what size to cut pieces for paper piecing. An easy solution to this problem is to premeasure the patch and add one inch for seam allowances before cutting the fabric. This eliminates the dreaded "Oh no!" discovery that you've cut the piece too small and it doesn't cover the patch. Any excess fabric will be trimmed off later.

For a Royal Palm label, cut the following:

Fabric	Cut pieces	Dimensions	Location
Tan	1	4" x 5½"	A1
	1	2" x 5½ "	A2
	1	2½" x 4"	B1
Medium green	1	2" x 5½"	A3
	1	4" x 2½"	B2
Dark green	1	2½"x 2"	B3

For example, for this label, Patch A1 measures 3" x 4½". Add one inch to each measurement and cut the piece 4" x 5½".

You may find it helpful to write the patch numbers (A1, A2, etc.) on small self-stick notes and put them on each patch of fabric as you cut (Fig. 30). This helps keep the pieces straight and organized as you work.

Make a paper copy of both units (Fig. 31) of the label pattern on page 92. Notice the pattern is divided into two pieces. That isn't a mistake. Each side will be pieced separately and then the two will be sewn together. Trim excess paper to approximately ¼" away from the sewing lines (Fig. 32).

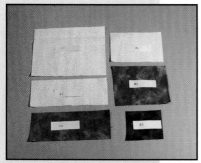

Fig. 30. Pieces cut out and labeled, ready for sewing.

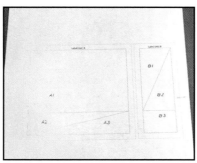

Fig. 31. Label before it is cut into two pieces.

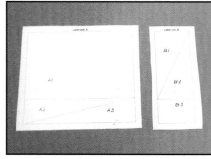

Fig. 32. Label after it is cut into two pieces and trimmed to approximately ¼" from the sewing line.

Paper Piecing Directions

1. On the unprinted side of the paper foundation, position the first piece of fabric (piece A1 - tan) over the Number 1 area (Fig. 33). With the printed side of the paper facing you, hold the unit up to a light source and make sure the fabric covers the entire area plus a ¼" seam allowance. Pin the piece in place, using a flower head pin, or you may prefer to attach the piece with a dab of glue from a glue stick.

2. Place the foundation, fabric side down, on a cutting mat. Place a postcard along the sewing line between A1 and A2 and fold the foundation back along the postcard (Fig. 34).

3. Place the Add-A-Quarter ruler on the foundation so the lip is pushed up next to the crease and the postcard. Using a rotary cutter, trim any excess fabric (Fig. 35). The Add-A-Quarter ruler gives an accurate ¼" seam allowance. (If you don't have this ruler, see page 91 to make a ruler like this one.)

4. Place the second piece of fabric (piece A2 – tan) with right sides together along the edge of the first piece. Holding the foundation and fabric up to a light source, gently flip the piece over and check to see if it covers the entire area plus the seam allowance. Don't neglect this step; it will prevent ripping!

5. With fabrics in place, flip the foundation over to the printed side of the paper and sew on the line between piece A1 and piece A2 (Fig. 36). Extend the stitching line slightly before and after the printed line. This will help prevent the stitching from coming out. Make sure to have a 90/14 needle in your sewing machine and set the stitch length at 1.5. It also helps to use an open toe foot which allows you to see the line without difficulty.

6. Remove from the sewing machine and place the foundation printed side down. Fold back patch A2 and press with a hot iron (no steam!) Move the foundation to a firm surface. While holding the fabric in place, run a wooden iron along the seam to help the seam lay flat.

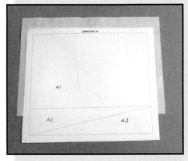

Fig. 33. Fabric placed on A1 piece.

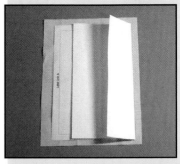

Fig. 34. Postcard placed along the sewing line between A1 and A2; foundation flipped back.

Fig. 35. Place Add-A-Quarter ruler along the edge and trim the fabric.

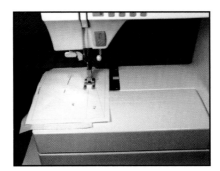

Fig. 36. Sew on the line between pieces A1 and A2. Seeing the sewing line is easier if you use an open toe foot.

Note: After pressing with a hot, dry iron, a wooden iron is used to make sure the seam is pressed open and is flat.

7. Place foundation, fabric side down, on a cutting mat. Place postcard along the sewing line between A2 and A3, and fold the foundation back along the postcard (Fig. 37).

8. As in step 3, position an Add-A-Quarter ruler on the foundation so the lip is pushed up next to the crease. As before, use a rotary cutter to trim excess fabric (Fig. 38).

9. Align the next fabric patch (A3 – medium green), right sides together, along the trimmed edge (Fig. 39). Flip the foundation over to expose the printed side and sew on the line between piece A2 and A3.

Fig. 37. A postcard is placed along line between pieces A2 and A3 and the foundation is flipped back along the postcard.

Fig. 38. Excess fabric is trimmed.

Fig. 39. Align fabric piece A3 with the edge of A2. Flip to make sure it covers the foundation before sewing.

10. Section A is now finished. Trim the foundation ¼" away from the stitching line (Fig. 40). STOP! Make sure you are trimming ¼" away from the stitching line, not on the line! Do not remove the paper from the block at this point.

Sew the B section in the same manner the A section was sewn. When the B section is finished, trim ¼" from the sewing line as you did in section A (Fig. 41).

11. Sew section A to section B (Fig. 42). Press with a hot iron without steam.

Fig. 40. Trim Unit A ¼" from the sewing line.

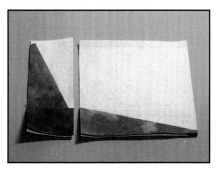

Fig. 41. Section A and section B, trimmed and ready to pin together and sew.

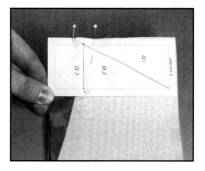

Fig. 42. Section A and section B pinned and ready to sew.

When the two sections are sewn together, the paper should still be on the back of the label. Don't tear the paper off yet. The paper should remain on the back of the block until the quilt is finished. To help the seam lay flat, though, you may find it helpful to remove the paper from the seam allowance between the two sections (Fig. 43).

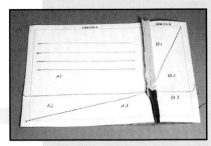

Fig. 43. Paper is removed from the center seam between units and the seam is pressed open. Lines are drawn on the back of the label.

Writing on Your Label

The paper on the back will aid you in writing on the quilt label. Using a ruler and a black permanent marking pen, draw four lines spaced approximately 1-1½" apart on the paper backing. Before marking on paper, test your marking pen. Make sure it will not bleed through to your fabric.

Flip the label over and lay on a white surface, such as a blank piece of paper. Using a fine tip permanent maker, write the following:

Line one: your name
Line two: your address
Line three: phone number (e-mail address)
Line four: name of the quilt, year made,
Line five: (You might even want to add that you made the quilt from the book *Floral Illusions*.)

Susie Smith
1500 Main Street, Any Town, TN 38401
(931) 555.1212   susie@email.com
ROYAL PALM made in 2001.
Made from the book "*Floral Illusions*" by Karen Combs

Once the label is finished, remove the paper. Since a larger needle and smaller thread length was used, tearing the paper off will be fairly easy.

Pinning Techniques

Often quilters have trouble matching the seams in paper piecing. That's a shame since paper piecing gives very accurate points, and not having seams line up can spoil the effect.

If you have trouble with seams or other areas matching, using the following pinning technique promises perfectly matched seams:

Place a pin into the first unit at a spot you wish to match (Fig. 44).

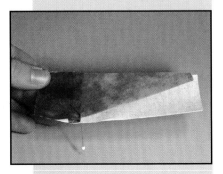

Fig. 44.

Put the pin into the second unit, making sure it is correctly placed (Fig. 45).

Place the two pieces right sides together, and holding the pin straight, squeeze the pieces together. It is important not to shift the pin, but to hold it straight.

Place a pin parallel to the stitching line, just below the first pin (Fig. 46). After inserting the parallel pin, remove the first pin.

You can also pin on either side of your matching point and remove the center pin (Fig. 47).

Pin the ends of the unit and sew (Fig. 48).

Repeat with other areas of the block you wish to match. When all the areas have been matched, remove the first pins and sew. Remove pins only after your needle has crossed the seams that are matched. This will give you perfectly matched seams (Fig. 49).

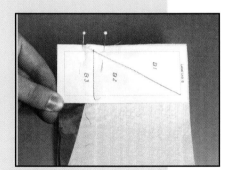

Fig. 45.

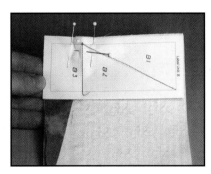

Fig. 46.

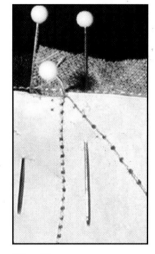

Fig. 47.

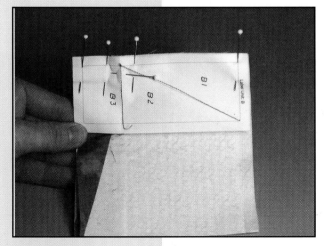

Fig. 48.

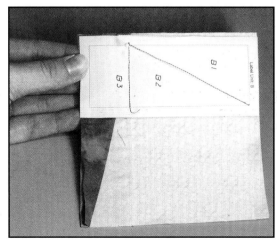

Fig. 49.

"Flowers always make people better, happier, and more helpful; they are sunshine, food, and medicine to the soul."

- Luther Burbank

Traditional Piecing

You may prefer to traditionally machine piece your blocks rather than paper piece them. Before you start sewing, review the sewing hints and suggestions to assure an accurate block.

Sewing machine – recently cleaned, tuned up, and threaded with off-white thread.

Sewing machine needles – For standard machine piecing, use a universal needle, size 80/12. You can also use a denim needle, size 70/10 which leaves a finer hole when piecing.

Iron – Steam is optional.

Rotary cutter and mat

Rotary rulers – sizes 6" x 6", 6" x 12", 9" x 9", 6" x 24"

Seam ripper

Straight pins – fine and with glass heads. These are sharp and glide through the fabric.

Fabric – 100% cotton. Use the best quality fabric you can find.

Seam Allowances

Stitching a precise ¼" seam is essential if you don't want to be disappointed with the results of your sewing time and efforts. When the seam allowance is incorrect, pieces won't fit, blocks will be the wrong size, and quilts won't lie or hang straight.

You may have heard that seam allowances don't matter as long as they are consistent. This may be true for simple blocks such as Nine-Patch or a Log Cabin; however, blocks that have many seams or points simply won't work unless the seams are an accurate ¼".

Before sewing any blocks, give yourself a sewing test and practice stitching a ¼" seam:

1. Using any fabric, cut two 2½" x 4½" rectangles.

2. Stitch the two rectangles together by stitching along the long sides.

3. Press the center seams open.

4. Measure the patch; it should measure exactly 4½" square (Fig. 50). If it does not, check your seam allowance.

If you have been using the right edge of your presser foot as a guide, you may be surprised to find that your foot is not ¼".

Helpful hints for stitching an accurate ¼" seam:
- Attach painter's tape or "mole skin" to your sewing machine to act as a guide for your fabric.
- Try moving the needle if that is possible on your sewing machine.
- Try using a ¼" quilter's foot.

Needles and Thread

Leading needle manufacturers recommend you start every sewing project with a new needle. However, since piecing a quilt takes longer than most sewing projects, it is best to change your needle after 8 to 10 hours of sewing.

Listen closely as you sew and with practice, you will be able to tell when the needle needs to be changed. You will find the sound changes from a smooth, gliding sound to a slight "popping" sound as you sew. However, even if you don't hear the sound difference, it's still a good idea to change your needle frequently. A burred needle can run your fabric and ruin your piecing.

Sewing machine needles come in many types and sizes. What should you use? The type of needle depends on the weight of your fabric and the kind of sewing you are doing. Needles are sized by a numbering system – the lower the number, the finer the needle. Be sure to buy good quality needles, not cheap bargains. The cheap needles may run your fabric and they often break easily.

When machine piecing, use a #80/12 universal needle. The universal needle has a slight ball point shape and is used for most general sewing on woven fabrics. You may also find that a #70/10 jeans needle works well. It is a finer, sharper needle that leaves a smaller hole in the fabric. Try each needle to see which you prefer.

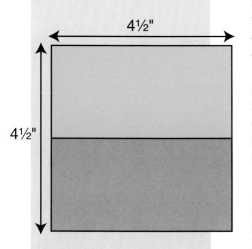

4½"

4½"

Fig. 50.

However, when paper piecing, use a #90/14 universal needle. The larger needle will puncture the paper and make removing the paper much easier.

To avoid puckering in your piecing, use a fine, sharp needle and a straight stitch throat plate. A straight stitch throat plate has a round hole for the needle as opposed to a wide hole designed for zigzag sewing. It is often an optional accessory for your machine. You will get an even, beautiful seam using a jeans needle along with a straight stitch throat plate. Don't forget to change back to the zigzag throat plate when you have finished machine piecing or you will break your needle the first time you zigzag.

Use cotton or cotton-covered polyester thread. Do not use quilting thread. Quilting thread is for hand quilting, not machine piecing. Don't try to save money by buying cheap thread from bargain bins. It breaks easily and in the long run, is not a bargain. Buy a good quality thread. You'll be glad you did.

Use a neutral thread color, such as off-white, beige, or even a light gray. If you use a neutral, it won't be necessary to change thread to match the fabric for every seam. The neutral thread works with every fabric color, even darks. For best results, use the same type of thread for both upper and bobbin threads.

Wind several bobbins ahead of time. As you are sewing, you won't have to take time to wind a new bobbin – just pop in a prewound one.

A good straight stitch setting for traditional piecing is 10-12 stitches per inch. For American machines, set your machine at 10-12 stitches per inch. On European machines, set the stitch length at 2 or 2.5mm.

When paper piecing, set your stitch length to 15-18 stitches, or 1.5mm. This tighter stitch makes removing the paper a breeze.

Matching Seams

Proper pinning is the key to accurate seams. There are right and wrong ways to use pins. Pin when necessary to match seams or to sew long seams. Pin perpendicular to the seam and never stitch over pins. Slip pins out of the fabric just as they move under the presser foot. (See Pages 96-97, Paper Piecing, for more pinning tips.)

Pressing Tips

It is important to press seams as you sew. Pressing helps match seams and ensures the finished block will be the correct size. Place your iron and ironing board close to your machine, or, if you like the exercise, place it across the room. That way you are forced to get up and move!

Use a well padded pressing surface or ironing board. A thick, light-colored towel placed next to your sewing machine makes a good pressing surface. The towel keeps seam allowances from creating a ridge on the right sides of your pieces.

Pressing is not ironing! Pressing is an up-and-down motion, whereas ironing involves pushing the iron. Ironing can distort the block and stretch pieces out of shape. To press correctly, set the iron down on the seam, apply momentary pressure, steam if desired, lift the iron straight up and move to another spot.

After sewing a seam there are several options for pressing seams. Whichever method you use, first press the wrong side of the fabric. Then give the front of the seam a good press.

Just a note about using steam. If you are paper piecing, it is not wise to use steam since the moisture can distort the paper and may cause the ink on the paper to smudge onto the fabric. However, since traditional piecing methods do not use the paper backing, steam can be used.

Pressing Options

Toward the Dark

This is the traditional method for pressing seams and is the fastest and simplest way to press. Press seams toward the darker color. Seams pressed to one side are strong and don't allow the batting to beard, or migrate, through and along the seam lines. This also prevents any shadowing of the seam. Shadowing is when the seam allowance is seen through a light fabric.

Pressing Open

Some quilters regard this as a controversial pressing method. Although it is a fairly new method and requires more time and effort, the results are worth it. Open seams produce a smooth quilt top that lays flat and hangs straight. It makes matching points a snap.

When paper piecing, you will need to press your seams open. This will ensure that the block lies flat and it also helps eliminate extra bulk in the seams.

If you use open seams, do not quilt using a stitch-in-the-ditch quilting stitch. Stitching along the pressed open seam breaks the piecing thread. Use stitch-in-the-ditch quilting only on seams that are pressed toward the dark or to one side.

*Rise and put on your foliage, and be seen
To come forth, like the springtime, fresh
and green,...*

— Robert Herrick, "Corinna's Going A-Maying"

Assembly and Finishing

Arrange the blocks as shown in the project illustrations. The layout stage is your last opportunity to move the blocks around before joining them. Before joining the blocks you may want to try the alternate designs provided in some of the quilt designs.

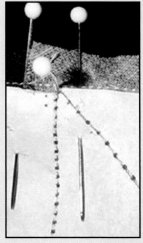

Fig. 51.

Joining Blocks

Identify several key spots (such as corners and points) and place pins through them so the pin passes perpendicularly through the sewing lines on both foundations. When the sections are aligned, pin on either side of the first pin (Fig. 51). Remove the first pin, keeping the two pins on either side in place.

Sew the blocks into rows, removing pins as you sew. Do not sew over the pins. Press seam allowances open.

You may want to refer to the additional pinning techniques on pages 96–97 before sewing your rows together.

Adding Borders

Borders add a finishing touch to your quilt and frame your work. Refer to the project instructions for specific directions on cutting borders. However, your quilt may measure slightly larger or smaller than the project quilt. These differences happen for numerous reasons and are not unusual. To ensure that the borders fit your quilt exactly, use the instructions below.

Measure through the center of your quilt, rather than the edges, to determine the size to cut your borders. Sometimes the edges stretch and measuring through the center is more accurate and will help prevent rippling edges.

Rippled edges are the result when the border is added directly onto the quilt, using the quilt edges as the border measurements. Since the edges of the quilt may be slightly stretched, or too large, the border then becomes too large, which causes the edges to ripple. Using the center of the quilt for the true measurement will rein the edges back into their original size. As you sew, ease the edges of the quilt to fit the borders, if needed.

Straight borders

Measure the quilt through the center. If your measurement is different than the cutting instructions for your project, use your measurements.

Add the border as follows:
1. Lay the quilt on a flat surface, smooth out wrinkles, and measure the length of your quilt through the center to determine the cutting measurements for the side borders.

2. Add ½" to your measurement and cut two border strips to that length. Sew onto the right and left sides of your quilt using a ¼" seam allowance. Press seam allowances toward the border.

3. Lay the quilt on a flat surface, smooth out all wrinkles, and measure the width of your quilt through the center to determine the measurements for the top and bottom borders (Fig. 52). Make sure to measure the side borders as well as the quilt top.

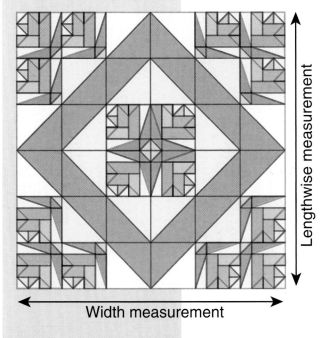

Lengthwise measurement

Width measurement

Fig. 52. Measure quilt top before adding borders.

4. Cut two borders to this measurement, plus ½", and sew onto the top and bottom of your quilt using a ¼" seam allowance. Press seam allowances toward the border.

If adding another border to your quilt, repeat instructions 1–4.

Mitered borders

Mitered borders are a little more difficult, but they are well worth the effort. A mitered border forms a continuous pattern around the quilt rather like a mat frames a picture.

You will not need to premeasure your quilt for this border; instead, use the measurements provided in the project.

1. Cut borders as directed. If needed, sew inner and outer borders together.

2. Fold each border in half to find the center point and mark it with a pin. Mark the center of each side of the quilt with a pin as well.

3. With right sides together, match the center of the border to the center of the quilt. Sew the border to the edge of the quilt, using a ¼" seam allowance. Backtack and leave ¼" free at each end of the quilt. It is important to have an accurate ¼" at each end. You may wish to measure and mark this point before you add the borders.

4. Repeat with all four border pieces, making sure to leave ¼" free at each end of the quilt. Press seams toward the borders.

5. Lay the quilt on a flat surface and fold it in half diagonally with right sides together. Using a ruler, place the 45° angle across the bottom of the border, so you can draw a line along the edge of the ruler from each corner of the border to the ¼" mark on the border (Fig. 53).

6. Following the pencil line, sew from the ¼" point, backtacking to the edge of the border. Repeat on all four corners, but do not trim the excess fabric. When backtacking, do not go past the ¼" mark.

7. Press borders, turn the quilt over, and check to see if the corners lie flat. If they do, then trim away excess fabric.

If the corners do not lie flat, you will see a crease in the fabric. Turning the quilt over and stitching along this crease should correct the corner.

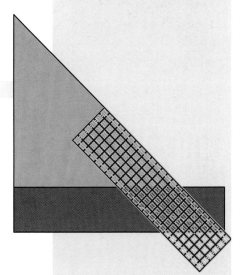

Fig. 53. Using the 45° angle on your ruler, mark the miter on the quilt border.

Removing Paper

The paper for paper piecing is removed after the quilt top is completed. Gently tug on the block from corner to corner and side to side to pull the paper away from the stitching.

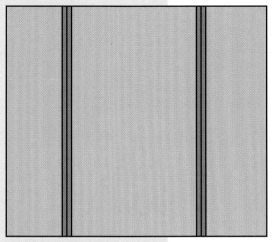

Fig. 54. Backing suggestion for quilts larger than 42" wide.

Backing and Batting

The third layer (or bottom) of the quilt sandwich is sometimes called the lining, but, is most often referred to as the backing.

Smaller quilts with widths less than that of a normal piece of fabric (42" – 44") will not need to have pieced backs.

If you do not want to have a seam in the back of a larger quilt, you can buy quilt backing fabric that is 108" wide. Your local quilt shop or a quilting catalog will have this available.

It's easy to piece a backing for a larger quilt. To create a pieced backing, cut two lengths of fabric equal to the length of your quilt plus approximately 4 inches. Remove the selvage edges from both lengths. Split one piece lengthwise and sew the resulting pieces to either side of the other length, using a ¼" seam allowance (Fig. 54). Press the seams open.

Basting

Basting is also called sandwiching. Basting a quilt is the process of securing the three layers – the quilt top, batting, and backing – together. It is important to do this task carefully so as to not shift the layers of the quilt.

1. Prepare the batting. It may or may not need to be prewashed (read the packaging for recommendations). At the very least, to help prevent fold lines, unroll the batting and allow it to relax for a day before basting. The batting should be at least 2 inches larger than the quilt top on all sides.

2. Press the quilt top carefully. Clip any loose threads and trim points so they don't show through the quilt top. After pressing, mark the quilting design if necessary.

3. Press the backing and make sure it is at least 2 inches larger on all sides than the quilt top.

4. Spread the quilt backing, wrong side up, on a clean surface. Depending on the size of your quilt, you can use a table top or floor. Being careful not to stretch the backing out of shape, secure the backing to the work surface. If you are working on a table or floor, use tape. If you are working on carpet, use pins.

5. Spread and smooth the batting over the backing.

6. Center the quilt top on the batting, right side up, smoothing out any wrinkles. Make sure the edges of the quilt top are parallel to the edges of the backing.

7. If you plan to hand quilt, begin basting the quilt sandwich with white thread. Make basting lines approximately 5 to 6 inches apart. Baste the quilt vertically as well as horizontally.

8. If you plan to machine quilt, pin-baste using size 0 or 1 brass or nickel-plated safety pins. Place the pins 3 to 5 inches apart. To avoid sore fingers while closing pins, use the serrated tip of a grapefruit spoon to grip and close the pin shaft.

Quilting

The quilts in this book can be hand or machine quilted. Whatever method and/or design you use, always begin quilting in the middle of the quilt, working toward the outside edges. See each quilt project for quilting suggestions.

Binding

Once the quilt is quilted, it's time to add the binding. Prepare the quilt by trimming the batting and backing even with the edge of the quilt top. Next, baste the edge of the quilt approximately ⅛" from the edge using a walking foot or an even-feed foot on your sewing machine. Add the binding as described below.

Attaching a Straight-grain Binding

A straight-grain binding is a binding that is cut along the cross grain of the fabric.

1. Fold fabric from selvage to selvage and referring to project instructions, cut needed binding strips.

2. Sew the cut strips together on the diagonal (Fig. 55). Trim seams to ¼" and press open (Fig. 56).

3. Fold and press the binding strip lengthwise with the wrong side of the fabric inside. At the starting end of the binding, open the strip and fold the end on the diagonal (Fig. 57). Refold.

4. Place the binding on the front of the quilt, in the middle of the bottom edge. Align the raw edges of the binding with the raw edges of the quilt. Leaving the first 6 inches unsewn, sew the binding to the quilt using a ¼" seam allowance (Fig. 58). Stop stitching ¼" from the corner of the quilt and backstitch.

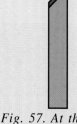

Fig. 55. Sew strips together on the diagonal.

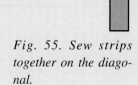

Fig. 56. Press seam open.

Fig. 57. At the starting end, fold the end on the diagonal and press.

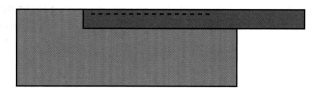

Fig. 58. Position the binding on the front of the quilt and sew.

5. Rotate the quilt to sew the next edge. Fold the binding up and away from the quilt (Fig. 59) and then down, even with the next side (Fig. 60). Stitch from the ¼" point and stop stitching ¼" from the next corner. Repeat for each side.

6. After you have sewn the binding around the quilt and have returned to the starting side, cut off any excess length and tuck the end of the binding into the pre-folded end (Fig. 61). This insures that no raw edges will show. Continue to stitch through all thicknesses until you have sewn to the original starting point.

8. Fold the binding to the back, over the raw edges of the quilt. The binding will cover the basting and stitching lines. Blind stitch the binding in place.

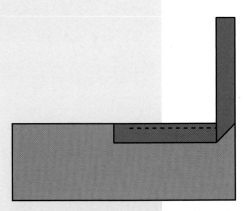

Fig. 59. Fold binding up and away from the quilt.

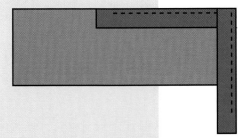

Fig. 60. Fold binding down, even with the next side. Stitch from the ¼" mark down the next side.

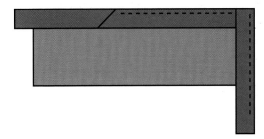

Fig. 61. Tuck the end of the binding into the pre-folded end.

Hanging Sleeves

Hanging sleeves, sometimes called pockets, are used when displaying quilts. A sleeve is constructed from a tightly woven tube of fabric. They are usually 4" wide and are two or three inches shorter than the width of the quilt. For a pleasant look, match the sleeve to the backing fabric.

1. Cut a strip of fabric as long as the width of the quilt (minus two or three inches) and double the desired depth of the sleeve, plus an additional ½" for seam allowances. Finish both ends of the strip (Fig. 62).

2. Fold the strip with wrong sides together and stitch lengthwise, using a ¼" seam allowance. Press the seam open and center the seam on the tube.

3. With the seam of the tube facing the backing, pin the sleeve to the quilt backing. Align the top edge of the sleeve with the bottom edge of the binding.

Fig. 62. Finish both ends of the strip.

4. Using a thread color that matches the front of the quilt, hand stitch the sleeve to the backing. Make sure to occasionally catch all three layers of the quilt. This will make the hanging sleeve stronger.

Labeling Your Quilt

A label provides a record of your handiwork for history (see page 96 for a label example).

• Always include the basics – who made the quilt, when and where it was made. Use full names for people and places.

• It is nice to add for whom and for what occasion the quilt was made.

• Information about the quilt name, the pattern, and the pattern designer is nice to include as well.

Write the information using a permanent pen and attach it to the back of your quilt. As with using any pen, pretest it on the fabric you will be using for your label. How fast you write will depend on how much the pens bleeds. Write just quickly enough to keep ahead of the bleeding. Always write lightly to protect the delicate points of the felt-tipped pens.

You can write your information on a piece of 100% cotton fabric, or make a simple block such as the label example on page 92.

Bibliography

Blockbase™ version 1.0, The Electric Quilt Co., 1991-2000.

Combs, Karen. *Optical Illusions for Quilters*. Paducah, KY: American Quilter's Society, 1997.

The Electric Quilt™ version 4.1, The Electric Quilt Co., 1991-1999.

Quilt-Pro™ version 4.0, Quilt-Pro Systems, 1994-2001.

Stash™ versions Fall 2000, Spring 2001, and Fall 2001, The Electric Quilt Co., 1991-2001.

Resources

Rotary tools, White glass head pins, Schmetz™ sewing machine needles, fabric, batting

Hancock's of Paducah
3841 Hinkleville Road
Paducah, KY 42001
800-845-8723
www.hancocks-paducah.com

Wooden iron, flower head pins, value tool, Add-A-Quarter ruler

Karen Combs Studio
1405 Creekview Court
Columbia, TN 38401
www.karencombs.com
(Online catalog only)

Quilting Supplies

Quilter's Attic
126 N. Main Street
Goodlettsville, TN 37072-1555
615-859-5603

Stitcher's Garden
413 Main Street
Franklin, TN 37064-2719
615-790-0603

Keepsake Quilting
Route 25B
P.O. Box 1618
Centre Harbor, NH 03226-1618
800-865-9458
www.keepsakequiltng.com

Nancy's Notions
Beaver Dam, WI 53916-0683
800-833-0690
www.nancysnotions.com

Machine Quilting

Barbie Kanta
1707 Santa Fe Pike
Columbia, Tennessee 38401-1570
Email: thepiececorps@msn.com

Quilting Stencils

The Stencil Company
28 Castlewood Dr.,
Cheektowaga, NY 14227
Fax Number: (716) 668-2488
Email: info@quiltingstencils.com
Webpage: www.quiltingstencils.com

Meet the Author

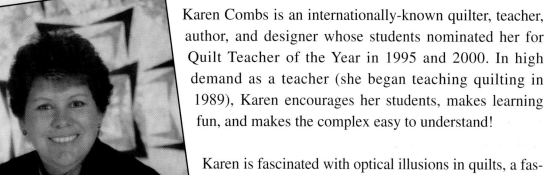

Karen Combs is an internationally-known quilter, teacher, author, and designer whose students nominated her for Quilt Teacher of the Year in 1995 and 2000. In high demand as a teacher (she began teaching quilting in 1989), Karen encourages her students, makes learning fun, and makes the complex easy to understand!

Karen is fascinated with optical illusions in quilts, a fascination that has become the subject of her many workshops, magazine articles, and books. She has recently paired with Clearwater Fabrics and Blank Textiles to design the Karen Combs' fabric line for quilters.

Karen's quilts have appeared in the Silver Dollar City Wallhanging Challenge and the Hoffman Challenge, as well as in many magazines such as *American Quilter, Quilter's Newsletter, Traditional Quilter, Traditional Quiltworks,* and *McCall's Quilting.* She was the Feature Teacher in the March 1997 issue of *Traditional Quiltworks* and has appeared on several TV quilting shows, among them *Quilting from the Heartland* (Series 700), *Quilt Central,* and *Simply Quilts* (Show 411).

Floral Illusions is Karen's third book with the American Quilter's Society. She is the author of *Combing Through Your Scraps* (2000)*,* and *Optical Illusions for Quilters* (1997), and is the co-author of *3-D Fun with Pandora's Box.*

She lives amid the rolling hills of middle Tennessee with her husband Rick, daughter Angela, and son Josh (when they are home from college), and a very sweet shih-tzu named Cocoa. Her hobbies (besides quilting!) include reading, yoga, walking, and photography. Karen included many of her favorite floral and garden photographs in this book.

Other AQS Books

This is only a small selection of the books available from the American Quilter's Society. AQS books are known worldwide for timely topics, clear writing, beautiful color photos, and accurate illustrations and patterns. The following books are available from your local bookseller, quilt shop, or public library.

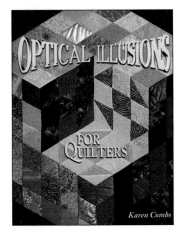

#4831   us$22.95

#5759   us$19.95

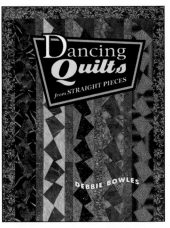

#6210   us$24.95

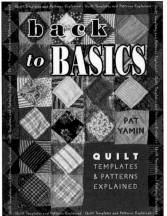

#6293   us$24.95

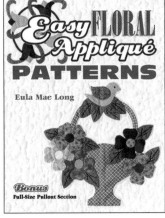

#6300   us$24.95

#6074   us$21.95

#6212   us$25.95

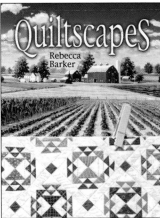
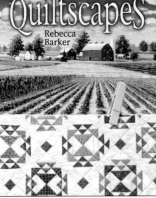

#6204   us$19.95

#6076   us$21.95